AMPLIFY LEARNING: A GLOBAL COLLABORATIVE

AMPLIFYING INSTRUCTIONAL DESIGN

DR. MATTHEW RHOADS

BECKY LIM

EduMatch
PUBLISHING

ISBN: 978-1-953852-87-8

We dedicate this book to educators around the world.

AMPLIFY LEARNING: A GLOBAL COLLABORATIVE SERIES

Amplify Learning: A Global Collaborative is a book series about integrating instructional strategies with EdTech tools to amplify learning written and compiled by educators throughout the world. Compiled and edited by two EdTech experts, innovators, and coaches, Matthew Rhoads and Becky Lim recruited K-16 educators from across the world to write a chapter of their area of expertise in integrating instructional strategies with EdTech tools to amplify their instruction and student learning. To learn more about the book series, check out www.AmpGlobalEdu.com for information.

BOOK 1 - AMPLIFYING INSTRUCTIONAL DESIGN

Within the first book of the series, *Amplifying Instructional Design* covers an assortment of engagement, collaboration, assessment, and feedback strategies integrated with EdTech for any classroom setting. By reading through each of these strategies and EdTech integrations, you will have a toolkit and repository of strategies that you can use to create any type of lesson within any classroom setting. Amplify your student learning and instruction by taking these practical and applicable strategies and integrations into the classroom and school by tried and true integrations from educators across the world.

BOOK 2 - AMPLIFYING AUTHENTIC READING, WRITING, AND MATHEMATICS

The second book of the series, *Amplifying Authentic Reading, Writing, and Mathematics* covers several instructional strategies integrated with EdTech tools to amplify student learning in these key content areas. Teachers will be provided with a toolkit of practical and applicable instructional strategies that can be utilized across any grade level to build student skills within in-person, online, and blended learning classroom settings. Strategies in this book will be illustrated utilizing a wide range of EdTech tools that are available in classrooms from around the world. Readers will be able to come to this book, again and again, to build their instructional toolkit to meet the needs of their ever-changing classroom and student needs.

BOOK 3 - AMPLIFYING STUDENT INQUIRY IN ROBOTICS, COMPUTER SCIENCE, AND STEAM

The third book of the series, *Amplifying Student Inquiry in Robotics, Computer Science, and STEAM* provides teachers with a toolkit of strategies to teach Robotics, Computer Science, and STEAM using a variety of EdTech tools. The instructional strategies and EdTech tool integrations illustrated in this book meet the needs of growing student skills across content areas that help power our modern world.

Teachers will see examples of how they can conduct cross-curricular lessons as well as put students in the position to learn the foundations of coding to create, empower, and even control robots. Readers will be able to see examples of the strategies provided in action as well as be provided with additional resources to help them plan and execute the lessons.

BOOK 4 - AMPLIFYING DIVERSE LEARNING NEEDS

The fourth book of the series, *Amplifying Diverse Learning Need*, provides teachers with a toolkit of strategies to differentiate and personalize instruction while integrating EdTech toosl to amplify student learning for diverse and multilingual learners. Strategies and EdTech integrations discussed in this book are geared towards providing teachers and diverse learners opportunities to provide optimal instruction within online, blended, and in-person classroom settings to meet students individual learning needs. Teachers will be able to take a multitude of strategies discussed back to their classroom to help further differentiate lessons through multiple modalities and EdTech supports and personalize them to meet each student where they are at.

CONTENTS

AMPLIFY LEARNING: A GLOBAL COLLABORATIVE

AMPLIFYING INSTRUCTIONAL DESIGN

Educators throughout the world are our best resources. Working together by supporting each other's practice amplifies our instruction and our students' learning. Living in an interconnected world allows us to connect more than ever and seamlessly learn from one another. As our world continues to transform and change at an ever-increasing rate, Interconnection becomes essential to providing our students with the most innovative and transformational instruction possible to meet the needs of all of our learners.

Education is evolving quickly, which means our tool kits must also grow. This includes the nature of teaching and facilitating and designing research-based instruction for our students. Technology has been integrated into almost every facet of education and has created classrooms without boundaries. As a result, the traditional brick-and-mortar walls of the classroom do not necessarily apply anymore. Learning can occur anywhere and at any time, which creates opportunities for teachers and students alike to engage in learning in ways that have not been done before in the "traditional" sense of classrooms.

What does instructional design look like in our modern world of education? Instructional design consists of utilizing strategies, curriculum, and technology to develop and create learning experiences for students. Educators write lesson plans that can be implemented into the classroom settings and utilize current research and strategies to meet student needs. Therefore, when speaking about instructional design, it is essentially developing instruction that can be delivered to students through instructional strategies integrated with technology. Currently, in classrooms across the world, we are in the midst of integrating technology into each and every facet of our instruction and classrooms, which is a massive shift in education. As a result, instruction can take place and move interchangeably among online, blended, and traditional in-person modes, transcending when and where teaching and learning can take place.

While technology integration holds much promise, there is much learning that needs to take place among educators. We now know the importance of using educational technology (EdTech) to enhance our instruction. Collectively as educators, we are being called upon to integrate instructional strategies with EdTech to amplify learning. Research-based strategies around instructional technology also show increased student opportunities for learning. Now, with such a variety of EdTech tools, we can amplify these opportunities exponentially like never before. As a result, learning can be limitless, creative, effective, and more efficient for our students.

"Education is the key to unlocking the world, a passport to freedom."

— **OPRAH WINFREY**

WELCOME TO THE AMPLIFY LEARNING: A GLOBAL COLLABORATIVE SERIES

Amplifying Instructional Design is the first book in a set of four books that make up the The *Amplify Learning: A Global Collaborative Series*. This book along with all of the books in the series provides a well-rounded instructional toolkit for teachers, coaches, and school and district leaders that can be utilized to amplify the learning occurring within their classrooms, schools, and districts. Additionally, the vast majority of the strategies and EdTech integrations discussed in this book as well as the book series can be implemented within almost every classroom setting imaginable. Overall, each book within the series focuses on integrating instructional strategies with EdTech in a multitude of different areas that span much of the skills and content that are taught to students in school.

- Book 1: Amplifying Instructional Design
- Book 2: Amplifying Authentic Learning in Reading, Writing, and Mathematics
- Book 3: Amplifying Student Inquiry in Robotics, Computer Science, and STEAM
- Book 4: Amplifying Diverse Learning Needs

PURPOSE OF THIS BOOK SERIES AND BOOK

Amplify Learning: A Global Collaborative series stemmed from the ideas and connections generated from a Global Professional Learning Network (PLN). The hashtag **#BetterTogether** comes to mind because as a collection of educators, we can work together across the world to amplify the learning of our students. As a result, both editors, Matt Rhoads and Becky Lim, decided to take this idea and crowdsource what we felt is a pivotal area in education: integrating instructional strategies with EdTech to amplify student learning. This manifested into *Amplify Learning: A Global Collaborative* book series, which is a collection of crowdsourced books on this topic from educators across the world who are teachers, instructional coaches, and instructional leaders. Together, we believe we can make a positive impact by bringing together our expertise to navigate and thrive in our ever-changing world of education through the work we are promoting in this book series.

Specifically, Book One of the *Amplify Learning: A Global Collaborative* series is on *Amplifying Instructional Design.* This book focuses on four key pedagogical areas that are student engagement, collaboration, assessment, and feedback that can be integrated with EdTech to amplify student learning. The strategies and integrations provided in each of these domains can help educators as they design and create lesson plans to meet their students' individual and diverse needs. Additionally, they can then be integrated with mainstream EdTech tools to provide top-of-the-line instruction within online, blended, and fully in-person classroom settings. Going further, the research-based strategies and EdTech integrations discussed in all three chapters of this book will provide you with a toolkit of strategies. Ultimately, this toolkit will help you design and facilitate your lessons in a modern classroom environment where learning takes place in both digital and physical spaces.

THE EDITORS

As curators, EdTech innovators, editors, and practicing educators, we both bring our own perspectives and experiences in education to this book. As editors of this book, our backgrounds are important to note as we will be providing commentary throughout each chapter in this series. While this book's purpose is to highlight the diversity of teachers and instructional strategy integrations with EdTech, we will provide our own insight throughout each of the chapters as to why these strategies and integrations are essential to amplify learning.

Matthew Rhoads, Ed.D. Dr. Rhoads is an EdTech innovator, an expert in data literacy and data-driven decision-making, and integrating instructional strategies with EdTech tools. At the beginning of his education career, he focused on blended learning and EdTech integration to amplify student learning. He taught English, math, and social sciences at the secondary level in special education and general education settings. Each of these opportunities gave Dr. Rhoads time to experiment and refine strategies and routines integrated with EdTech tools to amplify instruction and learning. Currently, he serves as an EdTech integrationist and coach that oversees six schools in North San Diego County. Additionally, Dr. Rhoads has taught at the university level with a focus on EdTech integration as well as supervised and coached new teacher candidates. His latest book is *Navigating the Toggled Term: A Guide for K-12 Classroom and School Leaders*. More information on Dr. Rhoads and his work can be found at www.matthewrhoads.com.

Becky Lim, M.Ed. As a mentor and leader in education, Becky aims to create a positive and sustainable impact across education! She is an innovative and passionate Digital Learning Coach that serves to support teacher and student growth. Becky transitioned from an elementary school teacher to a coach, where she currently supports elementary teachers district-wide. With a Master's in Educational Leadership and a graduate certificate in Instructional Technology, Becky uses her skills to drive meaningful EdTech integration. She works with educators globally as a Global Google Educator Group leader and leads #ECOpenChat (a coaches' open chat group and book study). More information on Becky Lim can be found at www.techwithbecky.com.

"If we create a culture where every teacher believes they need to improve, not because they are not good enough but because they can be even better, there is no limit to what we can achieve."

— DYLAN WILLIAM

DIVERSITY OF CONTRIBUTING AUTHORS

To ensure that we are broadening our skills and mindset, we intentionally handpicked leaders in education from around the globe to amplify their voices. Each contributing author brings their own dynamic style and perspective to their respected chapter. To grow our practice in education, it is critical to learn from educators outside of our network. We provide throughout this book research and strategies from a variety of different grades, content areas, and cultures. While each strategy may not directly align with the work you are doing in your classroom, we hope that you will find cross-connecting concepts and new ideas to support your students' diverse learning needs.

We have hand-selected eleven contributing authors from four different countries for the books in this series. All of them have expertise in the various areas the book series covers and the specific book that their chapter was selected for. Instructional topics such as engagement, robotics, collaboration, and assessment feedback are among a few of the contributing authors' areas of expertise. Each has a solid background in education and is well-known for their work with many years of classroom experience with students. The vast majority of the contributing authors are still practicing teachers. Additionally, they have curated many innovative resources ranging from templates, lessons, blogs, research, and books to teachers and school and district leaders within their professional learning networks. As editors, we made **sure** to do a lot of research on each author to make certain quality content and a diverse range of skills and expertise. We hope that the authors' unique perspectives support you in amplifying learning in your classroom.

MEET THIS BOOK'S CONTRIBUTING AUTHORS

For this book on *Amplifying Instructional Design*, the authors selected are all located in different regions of the United States, but carry the experience of teaching abroad and within diverse urban and suburban settings. Each of these authors carries years of experience in education working in the classroom, as instructional coaches, and as Directors of Educational Technology.

Debbie Tannenbaum (@TannenbaumTech), the author of Chapter One on student engagement, works as an Elementary School Technology Specialist in Virginia. After years in the classroom, Debbie switched to a coaching and co-teaching role where she has flourished. Her areas of expertise include integrating engagement strategies with EdTech to make learning stick for elementary-aged students.

Jeni Long and Sallee Clark (@jlo731, @salleeclark, and @jenallee1) are both co-authors of Chapter Two on collaboration. They serve as

Instructional Integrationists at the district level in Texas. Their specialty is with Microsoft-based tools and they have garnered international acclaim with the strategies and integrations they have been able to create with this set of tools. Their main strategy focus and passion has been on student collaboration for all ages.

Zach Groshell (@mrzachg), the author of Chapter Three on assessment and feedback, works as a Director of Educational Technology in Washington state. In his role, Zach coaches teachers on instructional integrations with technology. He is also responsible for ensuring that everything EdTech related is working across the campus. Much of Zack's research focuses on cognitive load theory, which is a major emphasis in his chapter that underpins the instructional strategies and EdTech integrations he incorporates.

Overall, each of these authors has written extensively and presented their chapter topics within blogs, books, research, podcasts, and demonstrations on YouTube. Additionally, they have spoken at conferences in the United States and abroad. Last, they practice the strategies and integrations on a daily basis in their role as educators. What they are providing is research-driven, applicable, and practiced strategies that work! Thus, as you read this, we recommend you follow each contributing author on social media to see their work in action and learn more from them and their professional learning community.

> *"A diverse mix of voices leads to better discussions, decisions, and outcomes for everyone."*
>
> — *SUNDAR PICHAI*

OVERVIEW OF CHAPTERS — AMPLIFYING INSTRUCTIONAL DESIGN

As you navigate this book, you may notice that the chapters are not organized in any specific order. This is for a good reason. We want you to navigate this book to meet your instructional curiosities and needs. Ultimately, you can always use this overview of chapters as your landing page to help map out your reading journey. Provided here are the abstracts of the chapters included in book one of our series. Each abstract summarizes the chapter and the instructional theme, including the instructional strategies and EdTech integrations discussed.

Each chapter incorporates a similar layout to provide consistency while still giving authenticity to each contributing author's voice. Before diving into EdTech tools and implementation, chapters will begin with research to give insight into theoretical concepts behind a strategy and validations of tools. Following the research will be the strategies and real-world application of each research-based pedagogy and EdTech tool integration. Provided below is a quick overview of each chapter.

- **Chapter 1: Student Engagement Amplified -- By: Debbie Tannenbaum**

The focus of this chapter is on student engagement, and it incorporates a variety of tools and strategies that can be utilized in all classroom settings. For engagement to be meaningful and authentic, educators need to become designers of learning. Mrs. Tannenbaum shares complex and highly researched strategies to support behavioral, emotional/affective, and cognitive engagement in the classroom.

- **Chapter 2: Collaboration Amplified -- By: Jeni Long & Sallee Clark (Jenallee)**

Collaboration is not a new term in education, yet there is much to be learned about incorporating EdTech and research-based strategies around collaboration into lessons. Jenallee shares many strategies to impact authentic collaboration. Throughout the chapter, you will find a running theme around the need for collabora-

tion in the classroom and workforce. The strategies and tools shared will prepare students beyond K-12 education.

- **Chapter 3: Assessment and Feedback Amplified -- By: Zach Groshell**

In this highly researched and applicable chapter, Zach outlines how formative assessment and whole class feedback can be deployed within all aspects of our instruction and in any setting. He covers four major principles that align directly with cognitive science research that are associated with formative assessment and feedback. Included in this chapter are discussions on delayed grading, online journaling, and individual feedback, and whole-class feedback, which establish a framework for assessing and providing feedback to students within modern classroom settings.

HOW TO USE THIS BOOK

When reading this book, the goal is to read and then come back to the chapters again and again for the content you would like to focus on amplifying your instruction. For this reason, we want you to narrow in on several different factors while you are reading the book to support your instructional integration needs in your classroom. Each factor discussed here is to help frame the context of how to use this book. Our goal is to support you in your journey to find the best instructional strategy integrations from educators across the globe. These four factors to think about while reading this book include educational context, instructional strategies, and EdTech integrations that can be adjusted to your setting; think less is more when selecting strategies and integrations, and watch out for notes from the editors along the way. Editor notes will provide analysis and commentary that may further support you in your journey.

EDUCATIONAL CONTEXT

Everyone's context in education is different. Each classroom is unique. From the students, teachers, instructional strategies, classroom setting, location of the school, and the resources they have available, all classrooms have characteristics that can never be completely replicated. However, most strategies and EdTech integrations can be adjusted and adapted to meet your instructional and student needs, though some may require more creativity than others. As you read each chapter of the book, consider your context in education and how you can adjust and adapt the strategies outlined to meet your students' diverse learning needs.

STRATEGIES AND EDTECH INTEGRATIONS CAN BE ADJUSTED

As discussed in the educational context, we wanted to spend time providing an example of how instructional strategies and EdTech integrations can be adjusted to almost any classroom setting. Depending on the setting you are in, strategies and integrations may appear different in online, blended, and traditional in-person settings.

An example of a strategy and EdTech integration appearing differently in multiple settings is the reciprocal teaching strategy, which can be integrated with interactive slides and recording tools within blended learning and online classroom settings. Reciprocal teaching is essentially broken down into four elements: Prediction, Questioning, Clarifying, and Summarizing. Using interactive resources like a Google Jamboard, students can see a problem and use manipulatives with textboxes in each to **predict** how to solve that specific problem. Then, a discussion ensues where students either write or state **questions** aloud relating to what they wonder about the problem at hand including the steps required to solve it. For the third step, students have the teacher **clarify** their understanding by modeling how to do the problem or providing an outlet or tool to help students clarify their understanding. Virtually, this could look like direct instruction, a complete interactive lecture on Edpuzzle, or working with a peer or online tutor. Finally, after the clarifying process is completed, students can **summarize** what they have learned and reflect on how they solved the problem. In a blended learning setting, reciprocal teaching could include both a synchronous and an asynchronous component where the first two parts of the reciprocal teaching strategy occur in person while the last two parts of the strategy occur asynchronously online. Or, if students are in an online setting, the first two parts of the strategy can occur synchronously, while the third step of the strategy occurs asynchronously allowing students to work on that portion of the task independently.

Overall, as seen in this example, there are many adaptations of specific strategies and EdTech integrations. Each teacher has their own resources, teaching styles, and lesson design in place, which may impact how strategies and integrations with EdTech appear in a classroom setting. Therefore, we must think about how various strategies and EdTech integrations work best for our setting, teaching style, and students. As you progress through this book, take note of how these strategies and integrations may have to be adjusted to best meet your needs, instructional setting, and students.

THINK LESS IS MORE WHEN SELECTING STRATEGIES AND INTEGRATIONS

As you learn more strategies and EdTech integrations, the goal is to pragmatically evaluate which ones will work the best for you and your students. Ultimately, when it comes down to it, be judicious in selecting the strategies because we want you to focus on successfully implementing three to five strategies and integrations versus trying on ten to fifteen strategies at a surface level. Have the "less is more" mindset and be aware that you can always come back to the chapters that have strategies you want to further investigate and implement in the future. This book is meant to be a reference for you. Get started by focusing on the strategies and integrations that will best amplify your instruction in your current classroom setting.

JOIN OUR GLOBAL COMMUNITY #AMPGLOBALEDU

To promote community, connectivity, and creativity on a global level, we want to take the learning beyond the pages of this book. Twitter provides opportunities for educators to connect, share, and grow from one another. Join our Professional Learning Network (#PLN) by following the hashtag #AmpGlobalEdu on Twitter. Our #PLN focuses on amplifying educator voices and opening the door for global transformation in education. We also want to learn from you. As you are reading, trying on new ideas, and discovering new strategies, share them with our community on Twitter using #AmpGlobalEdu in your post. Together we can amplify the learning of the greater educational community to impact student learning across the world. To learn more about the #AmpGlobalEdu community and book series, check out www.AmpGlobalEdu.com.

WATCH OUT FOR NOTES FROM THE EDITORS IN EACH CHAPTER

Throughout the book, you will notice notes from the editors. Each note is in place to provide commentary and further analysis related to the chapter's content. As editors, we bring our individual expertise and experiences in education to the table. As a result, our goal is to further support and help you integrate strategies and EdTech tools within your classroom setting. We will provide additional ideas, perspectives,

and resources relating to the content being discussed in each chapter. When you see a speaker or amplification symbol in the book that says "from the editors," this is what we are referring to here. Editor notes will arrive throughout and at the end of each chapter. Ultimately, our goal is to amplify the content discussed in the chapter. We do not want to take away from anything our contributing authors wrote. Rather, we are providing additional content and editorials to amplify your educator toolkit of EdTech strategies.

CHECK OUT ADDITIONAL EDTECH STRATEGIES FROM EDUCATORS AROUND THE WORLD

At the conclusion of each chapter, you will also notice strategies and tools from educators across the world. Each of these notes outlines a particular strategy and EdTech tool integration. We wanted to provide opportunities to include more voices and expertise to amplify the content discussed in this book. Each strategy is a stand-alone concept but can be used in varying capacities.

MOVING FORWARD

Are you ready to amplify your instructional design in engagement, collaboration, assessment, and feedback? Let's turn it up. Throughout each chapter, we hope that you build connections with the contributing authors and find new strategies and EdTech tools to bring back to your classroom, school, and district. Taking a global perspective that is provided throughout this book and series will allow us to boost creativity and spark innovative approaches to meet the diverse needs of students. Decide on the method you want to take in absorbing this book's content, and prepare to be empowered with many new research-based strategies and EdTech tools. Be sure to spend time at the end of each chapter reflecting and determining the best use of each strategy for your specific classroom needs. Don't forget to use this book as a reference. This book is not to be read and put on the shelf but meant to evolve with your pedagogy from year to year as you continue to come back and hone your teaching skills from class to class. Turn the page to begin amplifying your learning!

"Technology should not aim to replace humans, rather <u>amplify</u> human capabilities."

— *DOUG ENGELBARTY*

Amplifying Instructional Design

Part One — *Amplify*

Chapter 1: Amplifying Learning with Student Engagement

By: Debbie Tannenbaum

United States of America

"For without engagement, true learning cannot take place."
-Debbie Tannenbaum

WHY YOU SHOULD READ THIS CHAPTER

Classroom engagement is at the heart of student learning. You should read this chapter to hone in on behavioral engagement, emotional/affective engagement, and cognitive engagement in your classroom. Debbie Tannenbaum recognizes that researching student engagement is beyond overwhelming. In this chapter, Mrs. Tannenbaum focuses on key strategies and components of student engagement that can work for all teachers, novice to expert.

The strategies shared in this chapter integrate the 4Cs (i.e., Collaboration, Communication, Critical Thinking, and Creativity), Yales RULER program for Social-Emotional Learning, learning cycles, student inquiry, and much more. Student engagement is not a new conversation for any teacher, but this chapter provides in-depth understanding of a few tried-and-true strategies for genuine student engagement. Schlechty's continuum of classroom engagement (shared in this chapter) identifies what it means to have authentic student engagement over compliance. The strategies shared, such as using Google Jamboard for Thinking Routines to promote critical consumption and creation, demonstrate rigorous activities that allow students to take ownership of their learning.

Regardless of the subject area that you teach, learning cannot take place when student engagement is not present. This chapter will walk you through understanding the different types of engagement, tools for authenticity, and extended activities to take student learning to a deeper level in your classroom. Pairing student engagement strategies with EdTech tools will open up the door for students to be lifelong inquiry-based learners.

WHAT IS STUDENT ENGAGEMENT?

"Tell me and I forget. Teach me and I remember. Involve me and I learn."

— *BENJAMIN FRANKLIN*

"Involve me and I learn"-- ask any educator about engagement in the classroom and they will share how important it is to make sure we engage our students. But when we drill down deeper and ask for specifics, responses can differ greatly. A general understanding of engagement can lead to inconsistent application on the instructional side. With so many "engagement strategies" at our disposal, it can be overwhelming to determine the best ones to choose for a given situation and why to choose them.

Figure 1.1 *Teacher generated engagement word web*

A note from Becky: Create your own class word web/cloud using tools such as Mentimeter.com or Google Docs with the Word Cloud Generator add-on. Allow students to share one word to describe what it means to be engaged in classroom lessons. The word web/cloud can be a form of a social contract to hang in your classroom throughout the year.

As educators, our goal is to help our students develop into lifelong learners. This is a passion that needs to be cultivated and nurtured. Our students come to school as naturally curious. Teachers need to take them wherever they are and find ways to build connections to what they already know. In a world where there are many distractions, this can be difficult. We live in a world where there is immediate gratification all around us. It is a world where most of us learn using Google or by watching YouTube. As educators, we could view this as a challenge that we have a lot to compete with. However, we could also view these challenges as opportunities. How can we use what interests our students and implement it as we work to provide engaging classroom settings?

This task is easier said than done. If we truly want to amplify learning, we need to amp up our engagement in our classrooms -- reimagine engagement. How can we open up the doors to learning for our students so that all of our students can not only access learning but also excel and thrive? How can we take tried and true strategies to engage our students and level them up using our students' interests? How can we create engaging learning experiences that promote creation over consumption? All of these questions and more will be addressed in this chapter.

"If we truly want to amplify learning, we need to amp up our engagement in our classrooms -- reimagine engagement."

So what is student engagement? According to the Glossary of Education Reform (2016), "In education, student engagement refers to the degree of attention, curiosity, interest, optimism, and passion that students show when they are learning or being taught, which extends to the level of motivation they have to learn and progress in their education." As this definition details, many factors lead to engagement or the level of student motivation to learn and make progress. It consists of not only behavioral aspects but also emotional and cognitive elements. We need to consider all of these elements as we design our learning environments. In other words, we need our students to buy into what we, as the educational salespeople, are selling.

In this chapter, I will discuss how to get students to buy or opt-in to the learning at hand. All teachers want their students to be successful and thrive. I need to prepare students for a world that we have not yet seen. In the pages that follow, I will share the research behind why engagement is so important. Together, with you as the reader, we will dig deep into the three aspects of student engagement and give practical examples to strengthen each aspect. Using that research, I will also share some of the top ways that we can engage our students and why those strategies work. Then, I will share hands-on examples of these strategies integrating technology into them. Student engagement is built from the learning environments that teachers design. In this chapter, I will discuss some new and some old ways to amplify your students' engagement. Use this chapter as a springboard to examine what student engagement means to you and then take action by:

- Connecting what you already know to the research shared and the strategies highlighted.
- Extending what you already know and consider how you can add these tried and proven strategies to your classroom setting.
- Challenging yourself to take a risk -- try something new and model your own vulnerability as you learn.

Taking action and trying new things can indeed be a scary prospect. As you undertake this important work, know that you are learning research-based strategies and embarking on a process of continual improvement. For without engagement, true learning cannot take place.

THE RESEARCH AND STRATEGIES

Do a Google search for student engagement and more than 700,000 results come up. Try Google Scholar and your results increase to over three million results. Clearly, there is no shortage of information out there about student engagement. Articles, books, and research are plentiful and in many ways, completely overwhelming. Ask any educator what they think engagement is and you would be amazed how many words that come to their minds. Rather than getting overwhelmed by the plethora of resources, let's start simple and look at the three aspects that educators need to consider when looking at student engagement: behavioral, emotional/affective, and cognitive. Using all three aspects of student engagement, I will then highlight practical strategies for you that will enhance student engagement and share how educational technology can be used to further amplify student learning.

Behavioral Engagement

Behavioral engagement refers to the behaviors that students demonstrate in the learning environment. As Bond and Bedenlier (2019) share, this type of engagement is composed of many behaviors. Do students participate? Do they persevere through difficult tasks? Are they well-behaved? Are they developing or have agency over their work? Are they actively involved in their learning? Behavioral engagement strategies help our students to engage in **productive struggle.** We need to captivate our students' interest in instruction and give our students the opportunity to learn through higher-order skills and scaffold these experiences for our students. Productive struggle helps our students to not only grow their learning capacity and retention but also helps them become more independent learners (Hammond, 2015).

Behavioral engagement is a byproduct of both student and teacher behavior; it does not happen on its own. Educators need to not only carefully craft experiences that promote the desired behaviors but model those behaviors as well. Crafting those experiences happens before students even arrive as teachers plan lessons and envision classroom norms. Unfortunately, knowing effective engagement strategies is not enough; educators also need to be able to implement them. I will focus more on implementation specifically later in this chapter.

Emotional/Affective Engagement

Emotional or affective engagement relates to how students react to their learning environment? Do they feel welcomed and valued? Do they view learning and their classroom positively? Are they enthusiastic and curious to learn more? Do teachers and students have caring relationships established? (Bond & Bedenlier, 2019). Pedler et al. (2020) found that "when students feel cared for and noticed at school, their confidence and motivation increases" (p. 53). As a result, building relationships and communities within schools can ultimately help our students build their confidence and increase their motivation to participate in tasks and classroom activities.

The fact that relationships matter is not a new concept. Building a caring classroom culture is essential for our students. It helps students feel comfortable taking risks and being more receptive to new learning experiences. Many people refer to this phenomenon as "Maslow before Bloom." In a report on Australian schools, Pedler et al. (2020) emphasized that "[educators] need to make sure our students feel safe, so that their minds are more receptive to learning" (p. 53). Hammond (2015) writes in *Culturally Responsive Teaching and the Brain,* "positive relationships keep our safety-threat detection system in check" (p. 48). Hammond (2015) shares how our brain is usually conditioned to scan for threats, but when positive relationships occur, this reflex is held off and we are better able to focus on higher-order thinking and learning.

Setting up a positive learning environment for our students is clearly important. In the pages that follow, I will share strategies that help reinforce the messages that all of our students matter, and building our relationships with them is an important key to foster emotional engagement.

Cognitive Engagement

Cognitive engagement deals with deep learning strategies. It builds on the foundation set up with behavioral and emotional engagement and takes students to the next level. This type of engagement is the one we typically consider when the term engagement is discussed. Are we setting learning goals? Are all students using higher-order thinking skills? Are all students engaging in collaboration, critical thinking, creation, and communication? Are we using strategies that promote these behaviors (Bond & Bedenlier, 2019)? Pedler et al. (2020) shared from a report on Australian schools outlining "the need to have clear objectives, set goals, engage in new technologies and collaboration, and experience learner autonomy, and ownership as important factors for developing cognitive engagement" (p. 54). Altogether, these facets need to be integrated together to establish an environment that harnesses cognitive engagement.

There are many strategies that we can use to scaffold cognitive engagement. As we consider best practices for amplifying this type of engagement, we need to evaluate what kinds of thinking we are having our students engage in. Ritchhart, Church, and Morrison (2011) of Harvard's Project Zero shares that "we as teachers must create opportunities for thinking" (p. 30). We need to ask more constructive questions such as asking students to use their critical thinking skills to analyze, synthesize information, and evaluate. I will delve deeper into ways to do this later in the chapter.

A note from Becky: Today more than ever, curriculums, sites, and districts are putting an emphasis on building relationships and emotionally engaging students in the first two weeks of the school year. This creates a facade that if educators spend two weeks on engaging students emotionally, students will be engaged for the rest of the school year. Regardless of this facade, student engagement should be an ongoing effort. Incorporating all aspects of student engagement into daily/weekly lessons will ensure that authentic engagement is taking place up until the very last day of school.

Measuring Engagement

Now that we have a better idea of what factors influence student engagement, let's examine the levels of engagement that students can demonstrate in our classrooms. Being aware of these levels will help us as educators to reflect on our current practices. These levels give us a snapshot of engagement in our classrooms. They begin a cycle of action research where we can identify areas that we need to improve and celebrate areas where we are excelling.

Levels of Classroom Engagement

Bond and Bedenliner (2019), Schlechty (2011), and Spencer (2019) have determined specific levels for classroom engagement. In Table 1.1, Schlecty explains the levels needed to look at how students will respond in different ways to varying tasks and look at the patterns students show in learning over time. These levels contain a continuum going from the ideal level of engagement to rebellion.

Engagement	Engaged students pay attention to the tasks because they find them meaningful and valuable. These students also demonstrate persistence and show commitment to their work by freely giving their time and effort to it.
Strategic Compliance	These students pay attention to the task because they are searching for some sort of extrinsic reward. As a result, they persist in working on the task until they have met the terms of achieving the reward and give their time and effort accordingly. Schlechty emphasizes that many times this is mistaken for engagement since students "appear" to be engaged, but differs greatly in student motivation and persistence.
Ritual Compliance	These students give minimal attention to their work and look for ways to avoid work completion. They get easily discouraged while working and only do work under the direct supervision of a teacher or an adult.
Retreatism	These students do not pay attention to the work and often try to hide their lack of effort. They do not show persistence, time, or effort unless forced through teacher supervision into ritual compliance.
Rebellion	These students refuse to do the work as assigned. They lack persistence and actively rebel against the tasks given in a classroom.

Table 1.1 *Schlechty (2011) Continuum of Classroom Engagement*

Schlechty (2011) continues that we need to view our work as teachers as designers of engaging work, rather than instructors. He emphasizes that we need to include certain characteristics to create engaging work. Depicted in Table 1.2, he shares that if we focus on these characteristics of engagement, we will facilitate more engaging learning environments for our students (Schlechty, 2011, p. 51).

Product focus	Students should be engaged in working on a product of some sort
Content and Substance	By building relationships with students, the teacher is able to personally engage with every student.
Organization of Knowledge	We need to consider the learning styles of our students as we plan the learning activities.
Clear and Compelling Standards	Not only do we need to have clear standards, but students should view them as meaningful and attainable.
Protection from Adverse Consequences	We need to remove the fear of punishment associated with failure.
Affiliation	Student engagement increases when students get to work with other students.
Affirmation	We need to provide detailed feedback to our students to show that we value their work.
Novelty and Variety	Changing things up for our students can lead to further engagement.
Choice	By providing our students choices, we give them autonomy over their work.
Authenticity	We need to design work that students find authentic and meaningful.

Table 1.2 *Characteristics for Designing Engaging Work*

Schlechty (2011) is not the only one to view engagement on a continuum or share ways to move from one end of the continuum to another. Bond and Bedeliner (2019) discuss how the engagement is separated into the categories of actions, perceptions, and thought processes that occur in the classroom environment by students. Then, Spencer (2019) also looks at engagement but views it as the middle ground between compliance and empowerment. Spencer (2019) argues that "empowered learners are engaged learners." When you add student ownership to student engagement, you have student empowerment. Like Schlechty, Spencer focuses on actions or shifts that teachers can take that will give students more ownership over their learning, which is depicted in Table 1.3.

Both of these engagement thought leaders, Schlechty and Spencer, focus on how educators can design their lessons to lead to student engagement. That leads us to consider how we can put these design considerations into action with our students. How can we, as educators, design learning activities that engage our students? With so many factors to consider, this can be overwhelming. We need to find strategies not only that honor these multiple considerations, but also facilitate the many aspects of engagement.

Inspiring Possibilities	Many times as we work towards incorporating more student choice, we provide our students a couple of options for assignment completion. This gives our students choices but limits their freedom to choose. Spencer (2019) suggests reframing these choices as possibilities that students can choose from if they need inspiration but allowing students the ability to choose what inspires them most.
Tapping Into Student Interests	Consider incorporating student interests into your instruction. Allow students to learn about areas of their own interest, rather than trying to make something "interesting" to them.
Assessing Your Own Learning	Have students embrace a design thinking mindset where they understand mistakes help us to learn. Give students opportunities for self-reflection and peer-assessment and involve students in student-teacher conferences as a way to assess their own learning.
Answering Your Own Questions	Empower your students to ask their own questions and find their own answers.
Critical Consuming and Creating	Help students to become critical consumers. Have them use the design process to create.
Adjustable Systems	We need to empower students to set their own pace as learners. Students need to have the freedom to choose the formats to share their learning and what resources best meet their needs.
Self Direction	Often, schools promote compliance, but if we want students to be lifelong learners, we need them to feel a sense of ownership over their learning and promote that in our classrooms.

Table 1.3 *Teacher Shifts to Give Students Ownership Over their Learning*

ENGAGEMENT STRATEGY INTEGRATION WITH EDTECH TOOLS

As we consider engagement strategies, we need to have a designer's mindset. How can we design engaging instruction? The strategies shared below are excellent places to get started. They are, by no means, inclusive of all possible engagement strategies. These strategies provide our students more agency over their learning, establish a caring culture in our classrooms that fosters learning, and focus teacher efforts on facilitating learning rather than dispensing knowledge. For example, Choice Boards, HyperDocs, and Project-Based Learning (PBL) develop student agency over their learning. Mood Meters help us to establish a foundation for our classroom culture while Thinking Routines promote future-ready skills like critical thinking and creation. All of these strategies support our need to design more engaging student learning experiences.

"Mood Meters help us to establish a foundation for our classroom culture, while Thinking Routines promote future-ready skills like critical thinking and creation."

Use Choice Boards to Incorporate Choice into Student Learning

Tapping into our students' interests is key. It is one of our most powerful tools in promoting student engagement. If our goal is to facilitate student learning, we do not need just one way to demonstrate proficiency. There are multiple ways that students can demonstrate their understanding of new knowledge. Choice boards are essentially a specifically designed graphic organizer that allows students different ways to learn and/or demonstrate learning on a specific concept. Usually, Choice Boards include nine squares, but you can include more or less if needed. The magic of a Choice Board is in its ability for differentiation and how it allows students to learn using their best learning styles. Educators can design boards that are more Tic-Tac-Toe style (three in a row) or they can use choice boards to give students options for selecting activities to complete (Reinken, 2012).

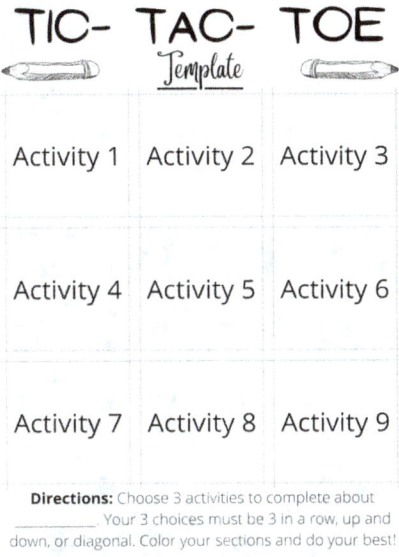

Figure 1.2 *Example of a Tic-Tac-Toe board*

To access your own Tic-Tac-Toe template, use this link: bit.ly/ampglobaltictactoeboard

Use Thinking Routines to Promote Critical Consumption and Creation

Thinking Routines are a set of questions or a brief sequence of steps used to scaffold and support student thinking. The premise behind Thinking Routines is that we, as educators, need to make students' thinking visible. Thinking Routines provide scaffolded models for students to share their thinking. It creates opportunities for not only students to think, but also to allow students to see others' ideas and thoughts. For example, the strategy See, Think, Wonder by Harvard's Project Zero (2019) is a thinking routine that requires students to observe, process the information they see, and then write several questions to further extend their learning and the conversation (see figure 1.3 for more details). It provides an effective means to activate prior knowledge at the beginning of the lesson. Thinking Routines are tools that teachers use to reveal that thinking. There are many thinking Routines, and each has its own purpose and function. Much like educators need to match activities to their learners' interests, Thinking Routines need to be matched to the desired thinking needed (Ritchart, 2015).

Figure 1.3 *QR code of See, Think, Wonder Thinking Routine from Harvard Project Zero*

qrco.de/ampglobaledu01

Use HyperDocs to Promote Autonomy and Inquiry

HyperDocs are digital lessons that can be customized to individual learners. They are not only interactive, but they also engage students in using the 4 Cs: Collaboration, Critical Thinking, Creativity, and Communication. According to Highfill et al. (2016), "a HyperDoc shifts the focus from teacher-led lectures to student-driven, inquiry-based learning, allowing the student to learn through exploration" (p.8). Both Schlechty (2011) and Spencer (2019) emphasize the need for creating HyperDocs and how this need puts the educator in the designer's seat. In their book, *The HyperDoc Handbook* (2016), the authors share Catlin Tucker's quote from her book, *Blended Learning in Grades 4-12,* "Teachers must be the architects for learning." Ultimately, HyperDocs put educators in the driver's seat because they can design multiple tasks and activities that are interconnected. For example, HyperDocs incorporate activities and tasks such as choose your own adventure, scavenger hunts, and personalized content creation options for projects that can be actualized for students. Through these types of activities, teachers have the ability to be the architects of learning by creating engaging lessons that promote student autonomy and inquiry.

Consider Using a Mood Meter to Assess Your Classroom Climate and Meet Student Needs

The Mood Meter is one of the four core tools of the RULER program. The RULER program was developed at the Yale Center for Emotional Intelligence. This program asserts that our emotions matter and if we focus more on the five skills of emotional intelligence, our classroom climate will benefit and student performance will increase (Yale University, 2021). The five skills of this program are:

1. Recognizing emotions in oneself and others
2. Understanding the causes and consequences of emotions
3. Labeling emotions with a nuanced vocabulary
4. Expressing emotions in accordance with cultural normans and social context
5. Regulating emotions with helpful strategies

The Mood Meter is a colorful grid that consists of four zones. Each of these zones represents a different group of emotions. On the x-axis, feelings range from unpleasant (left) to pleasant (right), while on the y-axis feelings range from low energy (bottom) to high energy (top) (Heart Mind Online, 2014).

- Yellow zone (top right): high energy and high pleasantness
- Green zone (bottom right): low energy and high pleasantness
- Red zone (top left): high energy and low pleasantness
- Blue zone (bottom left): low energy and low pleasantness

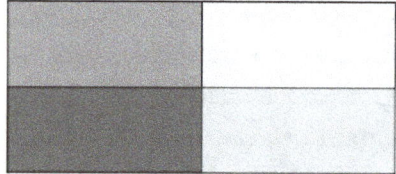

Figure 1.4 *Mood Meter visual*

The Mood Meter is one of the core tools for the RULER program. It helps students to develop an awareness of emotions both in themselves and others and begins the process of helping students to recognize their own and classmates' feelings and find appropriate ways to regulate them. This practice is essential as we promote both behavioral and emotional engagement and provides us vital insights to reach and motivate all of our students.

A note from Matt: Mood Meters can be incorporated using interactive slides, which can be the foundation for your classroom's social-emotional learning. The initial self-assessment, reflection, and opportunities to articulate how students feel can help create a classroom community as well as build your students' SEL skill set.

Use Project Based Learning to Create a Climate of Inquiry

Using Project Based Learning (PBL), students actively learn by engaging in authentic tasks and projects. Much like HyperDocs, PBL units differ from traditional projects because of how they include the 4Cs of Collaboration, Communication, Critical Thinking, and Creativity (PBL Works, 2021). When it comes to PBL, it is a common misconception for educators to focus solely on the end project and not the learning that takes place leading to a culminating project.

First, PBL units are not something extra at the end of a unit. They are central and integrated into the unit. In addition, they focus on a question or a problem that drives the learning. PBL units are inquiry-based and require students to discover answers through research, experimentation, and personal experiences. When students are able to integrate their life experiences, culture, and language into the project, learning becomes engaging and genuine. These units are student-driven and involve authentic tasks (Thomas, 2000).

STRATEGY INTEGRATION WITH EDTECH TOOLS AND INSTRUCTIONAL APPLICATION VIGNETTES

Armed with research and strengthened by strategies, we are now ready to supercharge these strategies (i.e., Choice Boards, thinking routines, HyperDocs, Mood Meters, and PBL) with educational technology. When we supercharge these strategies, we look at ways that the technology can enhance the learning that is taking place. Technology provides our students many opportunities for furthering engagement and promoting agency. When considering our use of technology, we need to look at how the technology is used within the learning experience and if the technology is transforming learning, modifying learning, or simply a substitution for an analog experience.

In this section, I will first examine best practices for integrating technology for each research-based strategy. Then, I will share an example of that strategy in action to illustrate how the strategy and integration can be implemented within classroom settings.

Use Choice Boards to Incorporate Choice into Student Learning

As discussed earlier in this chapter, Choice Boards are graphic organizers that allow students to choose from different ways to learn and/or demonstrate learning on a specific topic. Many educators have transferred this idea from an analog format to a digital one, primarily using substitution. However, in doing so, they miss many of the benefits technology can offer.

Figure 1.5 *Example of a student Choice Board*

To access your own Choice Board template, use this link: bit.ly/ampglobalchoiceboard

Best Practices for Integrating Technology

Bell (2018) in her book, *Shake Up Learning*, shares how technology can transform a Choice Board. Bell uses the Tic-Tac-Toe format in her version of a Choice Board. In this version, the middle square, square number five, is something that all students must complete. The Squares 1-4 all contain differentiated activities that meet the same learning target, while squares 6-9 contain differentiated activities that meet another learning target. Bell (2018) shared, "By forcing students to make the Tic-Tac-Toe using the middle square, I can design so that the other two choices will meet certain learning goals. One section might include exploration and the next might be for creation" (p. 74).

But the magic in Bell's Choice Board is where it is housed. Bell uses either Google Docs or Google Slides for this purpose. Both Google Docs and Google Slides allow the educator to use hyperlinks in their Choice Board. Adding hyperlinks creates a more dynamic learning experience for the students as they have the opportunity to access outside sources including ebooks and videos. In Google Slides, specifically, Tic-Tac-Toe boards become an all-inclusive package since you can create extra slides in the deck and link to each square to provide more information and detail (Bell, 2020).

Choice Boards in Action. My third graders used a Choice Board using Google Docs while learning about Ancient Egypt. They began by working on the center square. Box number five was linked to the Smithsonian Learning Lab where they got to explore a collection of ancient Egyptian artifacts. Students had the ability to choose one artifact to complete a See, Think, Wonder thinking routine using Padlet. By using Google Docs, I was able to hyperlink words in box 5 to both the Smithsonian Learning Lab website and the Padlet. All students got to choose an artifact that interested them and to see their classmates' thinking through the Padlet responses.

Figure 1.6 *QR code of Tic-Tac-Toe Choice Menu - Ancient Egypt*

qrco.de/ampglobaledu1

The blue boxes (1-4) in the Choice Board allowed students to determine their path for learning in their exploration of ancient Egypt. Students chose one of four choices, two videos and two books, to learn more about ancient Egypt and then asked to share three things that they learned in a Flipgrid. Once again, using Google Docs supercharged this menu. Students were able to access either the videos or books directly from the learning menu as well as access their classmates' responses in the Flipgrid topic.

The yellow boxes (6-9) helped students to explore the impact of an invention on ancient Egyptian culture. Students could choose from learning more about hieroglyphics, clocks, the Egyptian calendar, or pyramids. Then, students created 3-2-1 organizers sharing what they had learned. Much like before, students could access all the links for both reading about the inventions and sharing their learning on the Choice Board.

A note from Matt: Choice boards and personalized learning are key to help your students become engaged. Introduce Choice Boards by scaffolding your students into the various choices related to tasks and assignments that align with the objectives of the lesson. Students need a foundation of skills and instructions to then choose their personalized learning route.

I loved watching as my students' engagement grew using this strategy. They were not only empowered by the choices given to them but also loved the interactions possible through the external links. Definitely try out this Tic-Tac-Toe format as it is a great way to promote engagement in your classroom and begin your journey as a designer.

Use Thinking Routines to Promote Critical Consumption and Creation

Earlier in this chapter, I shared the research behind how learning is a consequence of thinking. Research shows that Thinking Routines provide students scaffolded experiences to make their thinking visible. Yes, these routines can be done in an analogous manner; however, technology provides us many ways to further amplify the use of Thinking Routines. When considering technology tools to use, we need to begin by identifying the type of thinking we want our students to do, and then we have to consider which tech tool would best meet our goal.

Best Practices for Integrating Technology to Implement Thinking Routines

There are countless tools that could be used for this purpose. I will specifically focus on three technology tools in this section. The tools selected provide varying opportunities with Thinking Routines, but they are by no means an all-inclusive list. In addition, all of the following tools are free for students to use.

Google Slides and Connect, Extend, Challenge

Google Slides works well with many thinking routines. My favorite to use it for is Connect, Extend, Challenge. While using Google Slides with this routine, every student receives an assigned slide in a collaborative slide deck to which all students have edit access. Why use Google Slides for this? By using Google Slides, every student is able to access and see the work of everyone in the classroom. It can help them find other articles of interest from their peers' slides. Students can also comment on each other's articles. It truly creates a collaborative and creative experience, where all students can share their critical thinking skills as they learn.

Google Slides and Connect, Extend, Challenge in Action

My fourth graders used this strategy while learning about the American Revolution. All students went online and identified a website article that interested them. Next, they added the proper citation, followed by how this article connected to what they already knew. Afterwards, students shared how this article extended their knowledge. Last, students reflected and added any questions that still challenged them.

Jamboard With the Four Cs Strategy

Jamboard is one of my new favorites to use with my students. It works well with many Thinking Routines. I especially love using Jamboard with the Four Cs. The Four Cs is a thinking routine where students first make connections to a lesson or activity. Next, they share what challenged them about the lesson or activity. After, they explain what key concepts or ideas are important from the lesson. Finally, they reflect and consider what changes in their thinking and/or attitudes have occurred.

Since Jamboard is essentially a digital bulletin board, students can be given edit access and add individual sticky notes during each step of the process. This allows students to see other student responses to further class communication and collaboration.

Jamboard and the 4 Cs in Action

After completing a coding unit using Ozobots, my third graders used the 4 Cs strategy to reflect. My passion for using thinking routines grew after supporting students who have needed to persevere through an activity like coding, because it increases their metacognition. Since this thinking routine was new to my third graders, I also decided to use Jamboard frames to scaffold the activity and add one prompt per frame.

The students enjoyed it, and this was a noteworthy way to summarize a fun STEAM unit. As a bonus, since we are teaching concurrently now, all students could simultaneously participate.

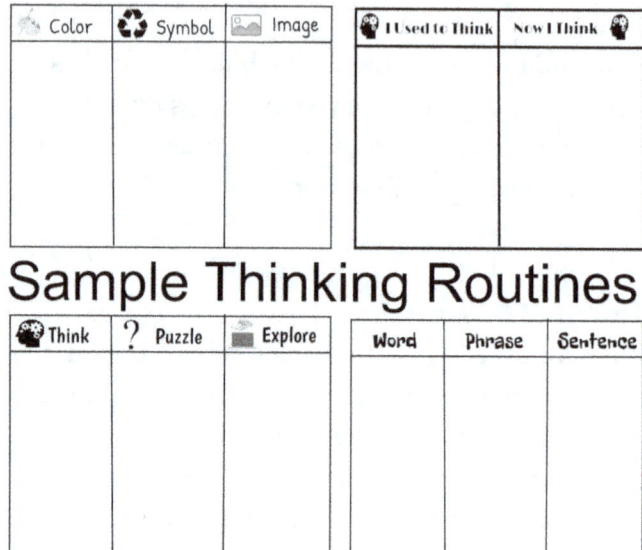

Figure 1.7 *Thinking routines in a Jamboard*

A note from Matt: Interactive slides incorporating Pear Deck or Nearpod are a way to solicit covert and overt engagement from your students. You can integrate think, write, pair, and share strategies as a way to have students complete a task, but also work with their peers in a collaborative fashion in tandem with interactive slides to amplify student learning. For example, the think, write, pair, and share strategy focuses on the principles of the Universal Design for Learning, https://udlguidelines.cast.org/, which has been shown to help improve student literacy and problem-solving abilities. Together, think, write, pair, and share has students collaborate, write, speak, and listen during a sequence of the lesson. We suggest using this strategy as a warm-up or during guided practice to engage your students in the content and skills you are teaching them to amplify your lesson.

Flipgrid and Circle of Viewpoints

Flipgrid's versatility makes it a fundamental application to use with Thinking Routines. The one I enjoy using the most with it is the Circle of Viewpoints. In Circle of Viewpoints, students choose a point of view and then share their chosen point of view answering a few prompts. Using Flipgrid works well with this because it allows students to not only share their "chosen point of view," but also to hear other students' "chosen point of view."

Flipgrid and Circle of Viewpoints in Action

During my unit on the American Revolution, fourth grade students learned to examine the American Revolution from different viewpoints. They got to brainstorm a list of possible viewpoints of people who may have had an opinion about the American Revolution, which includes the following list:

- Enslaved African Americans
- Native Americans
- Women of different races and classes
- The writers of the Declaration of Independence
- The signers of the Declaration of Independence
- George Washington and the Continental Army
- White smallholders, indentured servants, and tenants
- Patriots, loyalists, neutralists of different culture groups
- King George III
- The British Redcoats
- The French

After brainstorming, students self selected one viewpoint and answered the following questions on Flipgrid:

1. I am thinking of...the Declaration of Independence from the point of view of... (the viewpoint you've chosen)
2. I think... (describe the Declaration of Independence from your viewpoint)
3. A question I have from this viewpoint is... (ask a question from this viewpoint)
4. Reflect: What new ideas do you have about the topic you didn't have before? What new questions do you have?

Students creatively used the Shorts Camera to share their viewpoints. Shorts allows students to create videos without having a specific topic or assignment attached to the video. Since they were assuming another point of view, a video allowed students to 'act' and portray their understanding through a video. Plus, this way, students could listen to each other's viewpoints to expand their understanding of the American Revolution.

Mood Meter to Assess Classroom Climate and Meet Student Needs

As discussed earlier in the chapter, a Mood Meter, one of the core tools of the RULER program from the Center of Emotional Intelligence at Yale University, helps students to recognize their emotions and determine better ways to regulate them. This practice over the long term improves classroom climate, student relationships, and relationships between students and teachers. Mood Meters build both behavioral and emotional engagement in our classes.

Best Practices for Integrating Technology for a Mood Meter

Mood Meets open the door for technology integration in the classroom.

In fact, there is even a Mood Meter app on both the App Store and on Google Play (i.e., moodmeterapp.com). Creating anonymous responses or responses where the teacher is the only one who can see students' individual responses on a Mood Meter is challenging without the use of technology. Many Mood Meter tech tools provide vital information to the teacher while still giving students the opportunity to see where the class is as a whole.

One possible tech tool to consider when implementing a Mood Meter is Pear Deck. Pear Deck's draggable slides are ideal for this. The teacher can place a Mood Meter graphic on the slide and each student can place their dot where their current mood is. You could even follow the slide up with a text or a drawing question asking the student to explain why they selected the emotion they did. In addition, you could anonymously share how the class was feeling as a whole.

Another approach is to use a Google Form. Using a picture of the Mood Meter, students can identify which quadrant they are in and explain why. Each entry would be date stamped and could be analyzed in a Google Sheet. This information would be more private and be mostly for the teacher.

A final option is to use a Jamboard. Teachers can upload a picture of a Mood Meter in the background and students could add a blank sticky note to share how they are currently feeling. Like the other options, this data is displayed anonymously. Students could potentially move other students' sticky notes, so be mindful of that issue.

Mood Meter and Pear Deck in Action

After sharing a Mood Meter in Pear Deck with her students, one of my fifth grade teachers shared with me that her class became inspired. Why couldn't they make their own Mood Meters? They asked her if they could select pictures and create their own Mood Meters in Google Slides and then their teacher could copy them into her Pear Deck slides and make them draggable slides.

What an amazing way to boost students' emotional and behavioral engagement! Want to take a look? Check out — bit.ly/ampglobalmoodmeter.

Use HyperDocs to Promote Autonomy and Inquiry

Earlier in the chapter, we discussed HyperDocs and how they could be used to promote autonomy and inquiry. HyperDocs require educators to become designers of learning. There are five steps needed to create a HyperDoc (Highfill et al., 2019, p. 24):

1. Determine your objectives
2. Select which learning cycle you will use
3. Select your packaging
4. Build the workflow
5. Design your Hyperdoc

The first step is something educators do for all lessons. But when we get to the next step, we need to select the learning cycle. Many learning cycles can be implemented with HyperDocs (Highfill et al., 2016, p. 26).

- Explore, Explain, and Apply Sequence
- Workshop Model: Connect, Teach, Engage, Application, Reflection
- The 5 Es Model: Engage, Explore, Explain, Elaborate, Evaluate
- HyperDoc Model: Engage, Explore, Explain, Apply, Share, Reflect, Extend.

Educators need to choose the learning cycle that works best for their students. Afterwards, they need to consider the packaging, which is where technology comes into play. HyperDocs can be packaged in a variety of ways.. We can choose from Google Docs, Google Slides, Google Forms, Google Sites, or even Google My Maps (Highfill et al., 2016, pp. 27-28). Each one of these options has its advantages and disadvantages.

We need to consider our purpose and find the option that best fits our learning goal.

Best Practices for Integrating Technology to Promote Autonomy and Inquiry

Much like Choice Boards, Google Docs and Google Slides tend to be the go-to options. Google Docs allows you to create a landing page for your HyperDoc. Its features, like tables and the ability to hyperlink both words and pictures, helps to organize content. Docs are a quick way to make a HyperDoc, but it does not allow you to embed videos, only link them. You also need to consider how students will turn work in. Google Slides solves the video problem since you can embed videos inside of a slide deck. In addition, Slides allow you to change the page size and easily add shapes, like arrows. Both are viable options to consider while designing your HyperDoc.

After selecting your packaging, educators can then consider the workflow and determine how students will access the material. Will students get material from an email in their Gmail? Will you share the HyperDoc from your learning management system or Google Classroom? Finally, educators get to finish designing their HyperDoc. Please note that this is a summary of how to create a HyperDoc. Check out *The HyperDoc Handbook* (2016) or hyperdocs.co for a more thorough explanation and a variety of different ideas and templates to choose from (Highfill et al., 2019). We will share HyperDocs in action in conjunction with our Project Based Learning example.

Using Project Based Learning to Create a Climate of Inquiry

Creating a climate of inquiry is essential for PBL. We want our students to be involved in authentic tasks and PBL does just that. As we discussed earlier, PBL is not just a project but requires educators to intentionally design activities that require students to solve a problem.

That design process, much like HyperDocs, requires educators to consider many of the following factors.

First, like a HyperDoc, the project needs to be focused on student learning goals as well as including success skills like critical thinking, collaboration, and creativity. The project needs to start with a challenging problem or question. This problem or question needs to be open-ended and inspiring to students, while it also relates to the learning goals. To answer the challenge problem or question, students should consider what prior knowledge is necessary and use their questions to begin a process of inquiry.

Authenticity is necessary for the project. It should be a real-world task that someone in the field might do. In addition, students deserve opportunities to reflect throughout the project. Students should also receive regular feedback about their project so that they can revise and refine it. The project concludes with time given for students to explain their learning process and the potential opportunity for a public product that students share beyond the walls of their own classroom. Just a note, this is a summary of what a PBL should include; there are amazing resources at PBLWorks.org if you want to dive in deeper.

Best Practices for Integrating Technology to Create a Climate of Inquiry

Technology can be integrated into a PBL unit in many ways. To begin, technology is a fabulous way to build student engagement during an entry event. Consider adding a video to a slide deck or link to a museum or a live venue as your entry event. In addition, technology can also be used during the inquiry process. Students can use online resources to research as well as to take notes.

As far as a product goes, technology offers our students so many options for presenting their work. Students could create blogs, videos, presentations and so much more. But do not forget, with technology resources like Google Meet and Zoom, it is easier than ever to share your students' work with an authentic audience outside of the classroom.

A note from Becky: Giving students an authentic audience builds passion and ownership of learning. Culturally Responsive Teaching (CRT) includes bringing in an audience of voices, languages, faces, and life experiences that are representative of students in the classroom as well as the voices and faces of those that are not represented in the classroom.

HyperDocs and PBL in Action

As part of their study of oceans, fifth graders needed to study the impact of plastics on the complex systems of the oceans. For this PBL unit, we used a HyperDoc as the delivery system of the project and specifically chose the Explore, Explain, Apply model. The unit began with the driving question: *How can you, as an environmentalist, create a website that enlightens others about the impacts of plastic on the complex systems within our planet's oceans?*

During the entry event, students first watched a brief video clip showing one example of how plastic could impact the ocean, the Great Pacific Garbage Patch. The students then created their "need to knows" to answer the driving question. Next, as part of the **EXPLORE** section, students watched two additional videos on the impact of plastics on the oceans using EdPuzzle. After watching the videos individually, students came together in their groups to design a headline that encapsulated what they have learned. They shared the headlines on Padlet so that everyone could see one another's thoughts.

Students then entered the **EXPLAIN** section. They used a collaborative slide deck to take notes in their groups. To facilitate this, students were provided a variety of resources to use: videos, articles, books, etc. Students determined who in their group would focus on each section of the research and began their research.

After completing their research, students were ready to **APPLY** their learning. They created websites using Google Sites. While creating their websites, students were also given a choice on how they wanted to add a video to their site and an original image. After websites were created and published, we then had an exhibition so that all students could see each other's work.

CONCLUSION - AMPLIFYING LEARNING WITH STUDENT ENGAGEMENT

Throughout this chapter, we have explored student engagement from multiple perspectives. With so many opinions on what student engagement is and looks like, we began by sharing the different aspects of engagement. Also, you were challenged to connect what you already know to the research shared and the strategies highlighted. Then, we continued by sharing two different views of how engagement could be viewed on a continuum and research-proven ways to build student engagement. In this same light, we extended what you already know and considered how you can add these tried and proven strategies to your classroom setting. Using our newfound knowledge of the research behind student engagement, we identified five strategies to try to amplify student engagement. Next, we delved deeper into each of these strategies and shared the best EdTech integration tips and examples of each strategy in action. Ultimately, we want you to try something new and model your own vulnerability as you learn. Share your progress with us using the hashtag #AmpGlobalEDU. We cannot wait to see how you amplify student engagement with the strategies and EdTech integrations discussed in this chapter!

EDITORS' CONCLUSION

Each strategy shared in this chapter is complex while still encouraging teachers to become designers of learning. To avoid ritual compliance, or even worse, retreatism or rebellion, educators need to design lessons that support student authenticity of learning. Mood Meters can be used at any grade or with any subject to do a quick check for student engagement around social/affective engagement. HyperDocs incorporate the 4Cs and promote cognitive engagement while supporting behavioral engagement. Teachers, coaches, administrators, and any other adult working with students can pull strategies from this chapter to engage students in learning. The key behind student engagement is that teachers are designing the learning and students are doing the learning. Students should be asking questions, sharing their voices, and given choices in the classroom. Engagement goes beyond compliance.

Key Takeaways & Instructional Implications and Applications

- Student engagement starts with teachers becoming designers of learning and focusing on creating lessons that facilitate more authentic learning environments for our students. Following Schlechty's (2011) characteristics for creating engaging work, educators can create environments where students flourish.

- HyperDocs and Choice Boards allow for student authenticity, engagement, and choice while also bringing key lesson designs into the classroom. Both HyperDocs and Choice Boards can be utilized as components in Project-Based Learning.
- Thinking Routines with digital tools promotes critical consumption and creation especially in activities such as Connect, Extend, Challenge.
- Mood Meters using Peardeck or HyperDocs allow teachers to get a quick gauge of their students' readiness to engage in the upcoming lesson. Allowing students to create their own Mood Meter encourages student creativity and ownership of learning.

**Additional EdTech Strategies for Student Engagement
from Educators Around the World**

*Lisa Hockenberry -
USA*

Using Seesaw LMS to Heighten Student Engagement

When I first discovered Seesaw, I couldn't have guessed the path it would lead me down. I was the first in my school using it and I became a huge proponent of it. The tech tool really did transform how I had students work, and the engagement level went through the roof.

I used Seesaw in math stations for students to create and explain their thinking. Students would app smash creating a word problem and illustrating it on paper. Then the students would use that illustration to read the problem in Chatterpix. Students would upload the Chatterpix to Seesaw, but we didn't stop there. They would then solve each others' problems and comment on Seesaw about their answers and explain how they were able to solve the problem. I did several activities like this across all subjects: reading, science, social studies, and writing.

Seesaw completely transformed the engagement level in my classroom. Students were uninterested in the math games we played on paper, but when I started having them create in Seesaw to show what they knew of the concept, I saw lightbulbs and true engagement. It also benefited what I was able to observe and see who was successful in the math concept and who still needed some support. I continue to promote Seesaw as a digital learning coach and all its benefits for students learning.

Corinna Hathuc,
Ed.D. - USA

Pear Deck and Zoom to Engage the School Community from a Principal's Perspective

I found two tools that helped with engagement from a leadership standpoint: PearDeck and Zoom. These two platforms were used in the classroom, but using it as an administrator was helpful in engaging with students, staff, and parents.

- **PearDeck:** I purchased a site license to encourage teachers to find ways to engage students during distance learning. As an administrator, I modeled how to use PearDeck during staff meetings because our meetings were also virtual. I had engagement questions built in throughout the meeting so staff were able to have opportunities to respond in live time and also see their colleagues' responses. The feedback was saved into my Google Drive, and I was able to pull responses later to reflect and make decisions throughout the year. It was also a great way to take attendance without having to take attendance. In other words, Students are taking attendance through their live responses in PearDeck.

- **Zoom:** Traditionally at my school every Monday started with a school wide assembly filled with songs, announcements, and grade level cheers. I did not want this tradition to go away especially during COVID, so all assemblies were recorded through Zoom and uploaded into my staff Google Classroom. This allowed the staff to play the assembly every Monday, and the students still had the ability to sing along and hear announcements. Since last year was my first year as a principal at my school site, the video recording also allowed my students to "see" and "meet" me at least once a week. I also included PBIS student incentives for individuals who were upholding our school-wide expectations during distance learning. Every Friday I would have "Fun Friday" and teachers picked a student to recognize. Students were given a Zoom link to virtually have lunch with administration and during that time we would do scavenger hunts, do a directed drawing lesson together, or use PearDeck to get to know each other.

David Lerch - USA

Using Flipgrid to Engage Students and Families Throughout the Year

The 2020 year presented educators with one of the most difficult challenges of their careers. How can we engage students and families effectively when teaching remotely or virtually? The tool that came to our rescue was Flipgrid.

Using Flipgrid we were able to engage students and families on both a macro and micro level. Flipgrid was used to create special events like virtual Read Across America celebrations and virtual STEM night. These were done having experts record lessons, discussion, demonstrations, and talks and having students and families respond to them. Flipgrid was also used as a "get to know your teacher" activity where students could ask questions and teachers could respond about themselves.

On a micro level, Flipgrid allows reteaching opportunities with teachers uploading questions or problems and students recording themselves demonstrating their responses. Flipgrid also provided a measure of safety for students who didn't feel comfortable being "live" during lessons. The ability to record and edit video or only record voice allowed students to interact and engage in whatever way they felt most comfortable.

Chapter 2: Amplifying Learning with Collaboration

By: Jenallee (Jeni Long and Salleé Clark)

United States of America

"The ability to collaborate with others has become one of the most sought-after skills in both education and the workplace." - Jenallee

WHY YOU SHOULD READ THIS CHAPTER

Collaboration is essential in all industries and is continuously growing and evolving. Throughout this chapter, Jenallee will challenge you to incorporate new strategies into the classroom to engage students in authentic collaborative opportunities. The strategies support diverse learners in understanding their learning styles along with the learning styles of their peers. Throughout this chapter, you will gain a stronger understanding of ways to group students and give students a platform to share their learning with an authentic audience.

Many collaborative strategies shared throughout this chapter on engaging students can also be used with adults and colleagues to improve workflow. The chapter starts out with Jenallee (Sallee Clark and Jeni Long), sharing personal hurdles that they have overcome to better work as a team. Jenallee found that they improved as a team after they each took the StrengthFinders survey. Based on their findings, they then found ways to utilize the StrengthFinder survey with students to help them work better in small groups and with partners.

In this chapter, you will also read about gamification, authentic learning, and audience connections. The authors, two Instructional Coaches, share tried-and-true strategies that you can bring directly into your classroom to support all students K-12.

AMPLIFYING LEARNING WITH COLLABORATION

What does the "modern" classroom look like? It is not uncommon to see students working together in groups, pairs, or even working online in small groups. Collaborative learning and grouping students are not new concepts. The real question is, what types of activities are we using in our classes as well as what different tools are we making available so that our students can collaborate? Does your classroom provide opportunities to collaborate with diverse groupings? Are your lessons relevant and are your students creating for an authentic audience? Are you gamifying your classroom in order to boost engagement and collaboration?

Often, these opportunities are thrown to the wayside due to time constraints, budgets, testing demands, and lack of resources. Unfortunately, knowing how to collaborate does not come naturally. Students have to be taught the skills to collaborate. Collaboration has several benefits such as, "At its best, collaboration in the classroom can help students think more deeply and creatively about a subject and develop more empathy for others' perspectives" (Sparks, 2020). Sparks (2020) also shares, "at its worst, group tasks can deteriorate into awkward silences, arguments—or frustration for the one child who ends up doing everyone else's work."

When we teach our students how to collaborate, they develop higher-level thinking, oral communication, self-management, and leadership skills (Sparks, 2020). Collaboration also increases student retention, self-esteem, and responsibility. It provides an understanding of diverse perspectives and prepares the learner for real-life social and employment situations. The ability to collaborate with others has become one of the most sought-after skills in both education and the workplace. According to a survey by the Association of American Colleges and Universities, more than 80 percent of midsize or larger employers look for collaboration skills in new hires--but fewer than 40 percent of them considered new graduates prepared to work in teams (Sparks, 2020).

"The ability to collaborate with others has become one of the most sought-after skills in both education and the workplace."

A classroom is a small glimpse of the universe, and a classroom is an excellent space to replicate practices that can help students throughout their adult lives. As correctly pointed out by Henry Ford almost a century ago, "coming together is the beginning, keeping together is progress. Working together is a success." Developing a culture of collaboration helps create an environment where students are comfortable working together (Education World, 2019).

"Collaboration is an essential piece of the puzzle that completes the classroom."

Collaboration is an essential piece of the puzzle that completes the classroom. Students today need to be able to collaborate with each other by working in diverse groups, being both flexible and willing in designing solutions for a shared problem, sharing responsibility for the group's final outcome, and valuing each group member's contributions to the group (Trilling & Fadel, 2012). Ultimately, the goal of this chapter is to look at how we can foster collaboration in modern classrooms by integrating research-based strategies with EdTech to enhance and amplify student learning.

THE RESEARCH AND STRATEGIES

Technology brings pedagogy, good teaching strategies, ideation, and productivity together. It offers all stakeholders -- the parents, students, teachers, and community -- a unified location to gather information, to engage in quality learning strategies, to share and produce ideas together, and to create while seeking to apply solutions with a work product. Without technology, we would have to physically be in the same location to learn, we would have resources that are outdated as soon as they are printed, we would be limited to a physical audience, and we could only collaborate with those who are physically around us. Technology connects teaching and learning today to a global audience of students, parents, and communities. Technology provides us with opportunities we might not otherwise have. For example, we can attend meetings, watch a schoolwide spelling bee or awards ceremony, or even view district-wide student projects that might otherwise just be shown in school. Technology opens up a whole new world for us to connect. Our students are learning to use technology to create, communicate, and most importantly to collaborate. Working together is a vital part of the community and workforce, just as it is in the classroom. We are tasked with making sure our students are equipped with these resources.

Poth (2018), Foreign Language and STEAM Teacher at Riverview Junior/Senior High in Oakmont, PA, shares the following message around collaboration in the classroom:

As we prepare students for the future, where they will more than likely need to work with others as part of a team, they will need experience in developing the skills to collaborate, to problem-solve, to think critically, and to have discussions as part of the learning or decision-making process (p. 1).

Diverse Learners

We have the opportunity to create experiences for our students that are diverse in nature, experiences that support and celebrate different strengths among students in the classroom. Think about grouping your students according to their strengths. Look for ways to create diverse groups that allow each student the opportunity to showcase their skills. Everyone feels needed and important when they have a role that truly contributes and highlights their strengths. In diversifying our student groups, every student feels needed, that they belong, and that they contribute to the class. Hattie (2012) describes it is essential that schools focus on student friendships to ensure that the class makes new students welcomed, and, at minimum, to make sure that all students have a sense of belonging.

Authentic Learning Opportunities

We want to create authentic learning opportunities embedded throughout the lesson cycle for our students. Our lessons should bring real-world experiences and personalized opportunities into our classrooms. According to the ISTE standards (n.d), teachers are asked to design and develop digital age learning experiences and assessments for our students. They also motivate us to inspire student learning and creativity. Incorporating HyperDocs (as discussed in Chapter One) into your lesson design is the perfect vehicle to assure you are meeting these standards. According to Highfill et al. (2019), building HyperDocs requires educators to preview, review, and then leverage digital online resources often, efficiently, and effectively to model and teach students how technology can be integrated together. We learn best from interacting and communicating with others. Highfill et al. (2019) also found that when we, as educators, implement the newest collaboration tools in a HyperDoc, teachers give their students the opportunity to have a multitude of conversations where they listen, respond, discuss topics, build on ideas or comments, ask questions, and work together toward a common goal. Designing quality driving questions to embed in the lesson cycle is also a key component in creating authentic learning opportunities. Teacher questions allow for deeper problem solving and creative thinking skills for our students! Isn't that one of our ultimate goals as educators? We want to enhance the problem-solving and critical thinking abilities of students. Authentic learning opportunities intentionally designed by educators inspire students to seek solutions and think critically to solve problems that are relevant to their lives.

A note from Becky: HyperDocs are shared in chapter one and two because both contributing authors share a unique perspective for utilizing HyperDocs. We chose to keep both examples in this book because HyperDocs are versatile tools that can engage students and support authentic collaboration in the classroom.

Audience Connections

We also need to provide students with an avenue for global connections, virtual experiences outside of the classroom walls, and activities that provide audience connections. Authentic learning comes from creating lessons with purpose and from providing an opportunity for students to share their learning and creations with an authentic audience. That audience could be another class, parents, the community, or even students from across the globe. Providing opportunities for students to connect with other students, educators, classrooms, or even guest speakers can be done through various educational technology solutions, including Flipgrid or by participating in Mystery Skype activities. These activities open up a whole new world to students, offering them opportunities they might not otherwise get to experience. Having an authentic audience to share creations and solutions enhance the purpose for learning.

Gamification

Another opportunity that we will be discussing that fosters collaboration in the classroom is gaming. We want to facilitate learning that is relevant and intrinsically motivating for students, while also fostering critical thinking and problem-solving. The ISTE article "5 Ways to Gamify Your Classroom" by Haiken (2021) succinctly sums up gamification:

Gamification is about transforming the classroom environment and regular activities into a game. It requires creativity, collaboration and play. There are numerous ways to bring games and game playing into the classroom to promote learning and deepen student understanding of subject matter.

In this chapter, we focus on three gaming activities: Minecraft, Genially, and breakout activities.

Table 2.1 is a chart that outlines the opportunities that we have researched to provide an authentic opportunity for collaboration in the classroom. We will discuss in-depth strategies for implementing these opportunities in the classroom. We will also provide examples and elaborate on the ways that EdTech plays a key role in each of these strategies. We hope this chapter offers you a renewed vision of how to create a classroom that builds and fosters collaboration with an, authentic mission.

OUTCOME BASED COLLABORATIVE STRATEGIES

COLLABORATION OPPORTUNITY	STRATEGY	OUTCOME
Diverse Learners	⟶ StrengthsFinders	Knowing our students – grouping benefits
Authentic learning opportunities	⟶ HyperDocs	Collaborative opportunities in the lesson cycle
Audience connections	⟶ Flipgrid/virtual field trips Mystery Skype	Global connections, relationships, real-world applications, and problem-solving
Gamification	⟶ Minecraft Genially Breakouts	Challenging, critical thinking, problem solving, fun, and fosters a love of learning

Table 2.1 *Collaboration Opportunity, Strategy, and Outcome*

STRATEGY INTEGRATION WITH EDTECH TOOLS AND INSTRUCTIONAL APPLICATION VIGNETTES

As we step into modern classrooms, it is a joy to see our students learning together. We love seeing them collaborate and work together to learn and create. Reflecting upon our view of the modern classroom brings us back to creating authentic learning experiences with technology.

Collaboration with EdTech in Modern Classroom Settings

We have defined collaboration as a concept but have learned so much more in practice. In fact, we think that this word is the backbone to creating authentic lessons infused with technology.

What is Collaboration? We did not understand what real collaboration was until just a few years ago. It took us a long time to truly grasp the power of collaboration. It all began awhile back as our amazing leader and boss, Cindy Tucker, asked our team to do a book study together. Some of us were not thrilled at first. However, Sallee, being a former librarian, was giddy with excitement. The book we were presented with was *Strengthsfinders* from Gallup.

As we began to read this book, we enjoyed it! Who doesn't love taking quizzes about themselves and finding out which Disney character they are? I thought to myself, "what are their strengths?"

Finding out our strengths was very eye-opening and this book really became intriguing once we were able to see our co-workers' strengths. As each strength was revealed, we discovered much truth about each other. Each person's viewpoints, actions, and reactions became clear as we understood one another's strengths. As we work day in and day out with our team members, their strengths became more visible. One of the premises of the book is that we are all gifted with strengths that come naturally, and not only are they natural, they are also strong and it is easy to become stronger in them. Rath (2007) discusses how you cannot be anything you want to be -- but rather you can be a whole lot more of who you already are.

Think about it for a moment. What are you good at? Doesn't it drive you? Don't you just want to do it all of the time? And the things you struggle with, you have a natural tendency to cringe when it is time to do them. Who wants to go to work and only do the things that make them feel uneasy about every day? Who wants to go to work and do what makes you thrive, work hard naturally, and enjoy every minute of what you do? We know it is not possible to enjoy every task, but it is also not realistic to do only cringe-worthy tasks. When working on a team, would it be smart to harness each other's strengths to create the most productive work environment? So, in other words, if tasks were assigned by strength versus daily tasks that everyone completes, we all would be happier and more productive. That is exactly what we found.

As coworkers, we began to reflect on our survey results. And over time our strengths became more and more clear. Not only did they become clear, but we also found ourselves leaning on each other to perform tasks according to our strengths and joys. As Jenallee, we started looking at our strengths and our workflows and speaking honestly and transparently about them with each other.

Jeni's Top 5 Strengths	Sallee's Top 5 Strengths
1. Positivity	1. Connector
2. Arranger	2. Ideation
3. Communication	3. Strategic
4. Achiever	4. Empathetic
5. Woo	5. Positivity

Table 2.2 *Jenallee's Strengths from StrengthFinder Survey*

In looking at our strengths together, we see that we complement each other very nicely. We both like people and we are both positive. However, as shown in table 2.2, Jeni is strong in execution while Sallee is strategic. This is where we are able to help each other out and make our work more productive and enjoyable.

Sallee comes up with ideas all day long; most ideas are cray cray, and some good. She quickly creates graphics she conceptualizes in her head and makes them in minutes. However, after they have been created, they sometimes sit in her OneDrive, all alone and forgotten about as she has moved on to her next strategic idea. Jeni, being the arranger she is, checks the Jenallee shared OneDrive to organize and retrieve content. After organizing the content, she finds a great graphic regarding a topic that was recently spoken about. She will politely ask Sallee what she is doing with that graphic because people need the graphic (the relating strength is strong in Jeni).

As Sallee is being brought back to that conversation (because she has moved on and worked on five projects since), she remembers who needed it and why. Jeni quickly and effortlessly emails the content to the intended recipient with directions, explanations, and resources for more information. Jeni continues in conversation with the recipient until they fully understand the concept and are empowered to utilize it in their classrooms. During this time, Sallee has created five more projects, while Jeni has been in communication with the five other people from before and added to projects and offered suggestions on how to tweak them. Sallee tweaks, Jeni reshares. And the cycle continues.

Now, could Jeni and Sallee do all of this by themselves? Absolutely! Would it be as good? Absolutely not. Combining our strengths and working seamlessly together makes us empower more teachers and students! We are able to quickly solve problems for one teacher and share that data with ten others because we collaborate together.

Can Sallee communicate? Absolutely! Does she do it well? Yes. Is it difficult for her? Yes. Does it take her time to do it? Yes.

Can Jeni create and come up with ideas? Absolutely! Does she do it well? Yes. Is it difficult for her? Yes. Does it take her time to do it? Yes.

Once we stopped being jealous of each other's strengths and we found value in them, we began to help teachers faster and better. We feel that we are just now realizing what true collaboration is.

What is True Collaboration?

When thinking about collaboration, what does it look like? Listed below are a number of facets we should think about when developing a collaborative activity or task within our classrooms.

- It is seeing each other's strengths and truly valuing them in each other.
- Common passion or purpose
- Bringing together diverse strengths
- Communicating with others; discussing hard topics and problems
- Using combined strengths to create solutions to problems
- Putting solutions into action

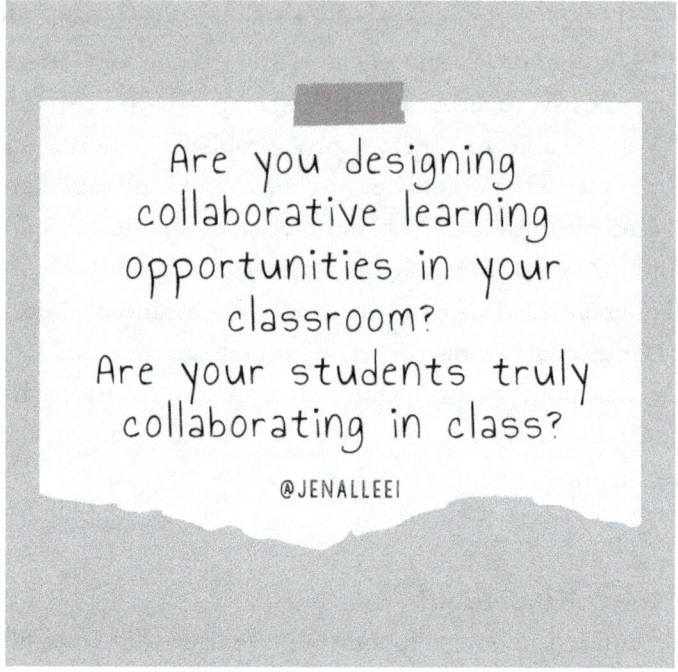

Figure 2.1 *Collaborating in the Classroom*

Are you designing collaborative learning opportunities in your classroom? Are your students truly collaborating in class? What if we took the concepts we have learned through real-life collaboration and applied them to our classrooms? Would groups work better together? Would students feel empowered and good at something? Would students have the opportunity to perfect their strengths? Let us take a moment to break down what we have learned and evaluate our processes for designing and organizing collaboration in the classroom.

EVALUATING STUDENT STRENGTHS

When creating groups in the classroom, we recommend building students up by focusing on their expert skills. Why not do a strength quiz with your students? Maybe conduct your own genius hour, a time for students to play, create, and investigate, to determine what students are good at. Give them the opportunity to feel proud of something they do well! Check out the QR code for strength assessment resources.

Figure 2.2 *A QR Code to Strength Assessment Resources*

bit.ly/ampglobaledu1

Diverse Arrangement

In creating groups, remember that students need to have a sense of belonging. In placing students appropriately in a group, we, as educators, can help foster friendships among students. We also have the opportunity to showcase students' strengths in a very visible and concrete way that group members can easily see. When we focus on the strengths of our students, they feel valued and in turn respond to each other in a more meaningful way. At times, students need to strengthen their weaknesses, but there are also times for them to flourish in the areas they are strongest in, and diverse grouping allows for this. Pay close attention to how groups are formed and make sure that every member has a role and an active part in the activity. Encourage group members to support each other and to celebrate the strengths of each member.

A note from Matt: Sweller (1988) recommends that for collaborative student work to be successful, focus on a variety of different variables that take off cognitive load during those activities. What is cognitive load and how does it affect learning? Cognitive load relates to the amount of information our working memory can process at a single time, which affects learning outcomes (Lechy & Sweller, 2008). Our social-emotions and stressors also come into play when thinking about cognitive load. Thus, when thinking about introducing students to any new form of content, instruction, activity, or collaborative, review the following steps:

- ***Review Task Complexity:*** *Refers to the complexity and difficulty of the task. When we add additional steps, it may result in extra cognitive load. If the task is not too difficult and too easy, additional actions by student team members not related to the task may result in more cognitive load because they are multitasking. Thus, teachers must analyze tasks based on the appropriate level of difficulty and rigor for their students to ensure the cognitive load is mitigated and not excessive.*

- ***Take into Account the Expertise of Students in the Group:*** *Students who have expertise in the content and skills being taught in their class will have less cognitive load related to the task. This is important when reviewing the final three segments.*

- ***Team Roles are Essential:*** *Team roles make it clear who has responsibility over the various parts of the task or assignment, which will eliminate the additional cognitive load of having to divvy out duties to teammates.*

- ***Team Size -- Three to Four Students Max:*** *The more members of a team of students working together, the more transaction activities that will occur among team members. Ultimately, this will increase the overall cognitive load inhibiting optimal performance. Thus, teachers should work towards keeping teams relatively small (i.e., four or fewer students).*

- ***Focus on Homogenous Team Compositions:*** *A lower cognitive load will manifest within a team of students if students have similar knowledge and skills related to the task.*
- ***Prior Knowledge/Task Experience is Huge:*** *If members of the team have prior experience working together or prior knowledge related to the task being asked upon by their teacher, there will be less cognitive load caused by the collaborative activities.*

AUTHENTIC LEARNING OPPORTUNITIES

As educators, it is our responsibility to provide our students with authentic learning opportunities. These opportunities should be relevant and meaningful and should increase rigor. Allowing our students to think creatively, encounter real-world experiences, and choose how and what they learn increases engagement and ownership of the material being taught. Students should also experience failure and success during these learning opportunities. There are a variety of ways to bring authentic learning opportunities into the classroom but one of our favorite ways is utilizing HyperDocs in a collaborative manner.

Using HyperDocs for Authentic Student Collaboration

Recently, Jenallee was honored to have Lisa Highfill and Holly Clark on The Jenallee Show! Lisa is one of the creators of HyperDocs and Holly is extremely knowledgeable about how to implement these amazing teaching tools into the classroom and is our inspiration on what the modern classroom looks like with the Infused Classroom model.

We had heard of HyperDocs but had never used them extensively. We are embarrassed to say this now, but we honestly just thought HyperDocs were documents with links in them. Boy were we wrong! We learned so much about HyperDocs from Lisa and Holly. Scan the Figure 2.3 QR code to see the interview with the HyperDocs Girls. You will see that this conversation motivated us to take a number of strategies and activities we love and make them fun, engaging, and collaborative for our students.

Figure 2.3 *A QR Code to The Jenallee Show: Live with Holly Clark & Lisa Highfill*

bit.ly/ampglobaledu2

HyperDocs can be utilized for students to collaborate in authentic ways. Students can collaborate within HyperDocs because they allow for students to take individual roles and work towards a lesson objective in a creative and authentic manner. Before jumping into these examples, recall that HyperDocs include the following features:

- HyperDocs offer the teacher and the students the ability to go through the lesson cycle. Each part of the lesson is built right into the document. It can be a one-day lesson, a unit, or a project lesson built out over time.
- HyperDocs serve as one central location filled with information for each part of the lesson.
- **HyperDocs are not just links.** They are lessons that connect background knowledge in the engage section and formative assessment in the explore section. They also consist of direct

teaching addressing formative assessment results, authentic application, and evaluation. Creating a HyperDoc helps ensure that we as teachers are going through the complete lesson cycle.

- HyperDocs can be utilized for individual and collaborative tasks and activities.
- HyperDocs can be used for gamification activities as well as providing students with a step-by-step sequences within a choice board format to help them demonstrate their learning in new and authentic ways

The first example HyperDocs can be used for is the collaborative task of navigating a virtual Escape Room activity using HyperDocs as a mechanism to take students through a digital maze of tasks and activities. Students are divided into pairs or groups and must solve a multitude of problems by going through a maze of documents, visuals, problems, and videos. Ultimately, through this collaborative activity, students have the opportunity to investigate, explore, and create their own meaning individually and as a group. Additionally, this may lead to students being engaged and taking ownership of the problems they are solving, which may lead to deeper connections and learning.

The second example of how a HyperDoc can be utilized collaboratively is during Project-Based Learning (PBL). HyperDocs can lay the groundwork of the project in a sequential manner and provide students within groups with each step for the group as well as individual group members. For this example, let's say students were investigating a series of documents relating to how too many satellites are being launched causing too much space junk. Then, students are asked to take a position on whether we need further regulations or not to stop satellites from being launched into space. Once a position is taken, their group is tasked to record a podcast that takes a specific stance on this issue. HyperDocs can be designed to allow students to investigate the same documents, utilize the same graphic organizer to organize their thoughts, and provide the directions on how each group can produce their own podcast. All of this can be housed on the same set of documents or slides whereby students can navigate with ease.

In a similar manner, this same example can be used to demonstrate how HyperDocs in a collaborative setting can create different roles within a group of students. One or two students may be tasked with writing the script for the podcast based on how the entire group collaboratively completed the graphic organizer after analyzing the documents. Additionally, the HyperDoc can lay out which students and how students participate in the podcast while the application supporting the recording of the podcast is hyperlinked directly on a HyperDoc.

Overall, HyperDocs seamlessly allow you, as the facilitator, to cultivate conversations, and thinking processes of students. Additionally, this can be done all while moving through the lesson cycle in a collaborative manner for your students to work together in fun, engaging, and authentic ways. Utilizing HyperDocs within the classroom makes it easy for the teacher to focus on integrating instruction focusing on the whole child, while also cultivating learning moments in a lesson cycle that is easy to build and implement. HyperDocs makes it efficient to plan and integrate authentic collaborative learning opportunities for students to drive their learning, creation, and connections with audiences. Want to learn more about HyperDocs? We suggest you check out Lisa's website that offers implementation ideas, templates, and more at Hyperdoc.co.

A note from Matt: When using Hyperdocs, teachers can incorporate the jigsaw strategy, which is a collaborative learning activity. When implementing the jigsaw strategy, a teacher assigns members of the group different resources to explore such as a video, podcast, or article. Then, after time exploring their assigned materials, group members share out their key findings to the group to either build further background knowledge or problem solve. Overall, this strategy gives students opportunities

to take on the responsibility to learn and to teach others in their group what they learned in order to complete a task.

AUTHENTIC LEARNING TO FOSTER MEANINGFUL ACTION

Students need a shared passion or goal to work towards. As teachers, when designing learning opportunities for our students, it is not enough to just say work together and create together. What good is collaboration without action? Action gives collaboration meaning. If students have to work together to plan and create just for a grade, passion can be void. If students have to work together to make a difference in their community, school, online, social media, etc., now we are tapping into authentic learning moments that bring collaboration to life. For Jeni and Sallee, their passion is empowering teachers to facilitate learning experiences for their students that bring about action and excitement for change. According to Campbell (2017):

When team members feel they are a part of something exceptional they are more than willing to work together to get the ball across the goal line. Collaboration works because there is nothing more meaningful, bonding or growth promoting than a shared win (p. 1).

Be strategic when creating groups: find students' strengths, passions, and goals. Group them well. Give students the opportunity to be passionate about outcomes that bring about action, change, and meaning. Ultimately, we feel that one of the biggest pieces of collaboration is action! What good are communication, solutions, and creations if we don't use them to bring about change?

"If students have to work together to plan and create just for a grade, passion can be void."

WHAT DOES TRUE COLLABORATION LOOK LIKE IN THE LESSON CYCLE?

We think it is all about how you as the teacher design your lessons. It is bringing a diverse group of students together to find a solution to an authentic problem with an action that can be implemented in a relative setting. That's a whole lot of words to say "to add effective collaboration to your lesson cycle." This is one reason we love HyperDocs. It allows you to use the lesson cycle of your choice to bring about learning. When we look at the traditional cycle, we believe that collaboration can begin during the application stage of your lessons.

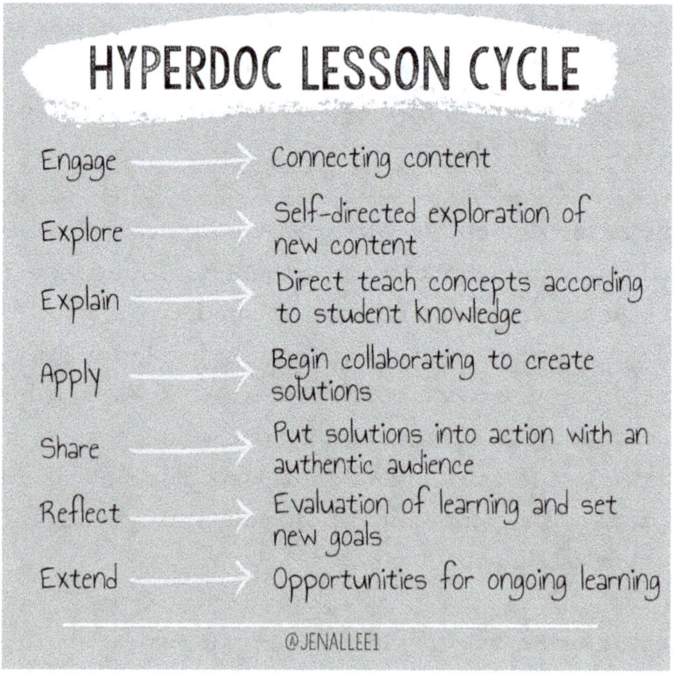

HYPERDOC LESSON CYCLE

Engage	Connecting content
Explore	Self-directed exploration of new content
Explain	Direct teach concepts according to student knowledge
Apply	Begin collaborating to create solutions
Share	Put solutions into action with an authentic audience
Reflect	Evaluation of learning and set new goals
Extend	Opportunities for ongoing learning

@JENALLEE1

Figure 2.4 *HyperDoc Lesson Cycle*

Before and During Collaboration

During the engage, explore, and explain sections of this instructional sequence, the teacher is connecting content and experiences with students. Then, they are allowing students time to explore. Finally, this leads to opportunities to assess student learning. During the apply section, students have a good working knowledge of the concepts and can put them into action. At this point, they are ready to discuss, plan, build, and connect this knowledge to action. We know that collaborating and creating mean nothing if action cannot be taken. We feel that it is imperative that meaningful action be tied into the lesson. Students are now ready to begin working in groups to collaborate and create solutions to quality driving questions.

AUDIENCE CONNECTIONS

What are you doing in your classroom to bring about global connections and real-world experiences for your students? It is imperative that we design ways for our students to solve problems, create, collaborate, and connect. In doing so we are meeting the ISTE and Common Core standards for teachers and students but also giving students memorable experiences that they might not otherwise encounter. Two of our suggestions for creating audience connections for your students are by participating in Mystery Skype activities and incorporating Flipgrid into your lessons.

Mystery Skype

In research from EducationWorld (2019), collaborative learning projects at an early age can help students boost their confidence and self-esteem, besides improving their sense of ownership at work. One example of collaborative connections is found in holding a Mystery Skype with another class. A Mystery Skype is simply a fun question-and-answer game between two classrooms. This can be done by each class taking turns asking each other yes or no questions in order to determine the location of the other class. The game can also be played by determining an animal or number that the other class has chosen. Typically, the lower grades will choose an animal or number and the upper grades will choose a location. Often, after classes have connected in this way, they will continue the collaboration over Flipgrid by becoming Gridpals. This is a meaningful way for students to discuss issues throughout the year that they are studying, such as holidays or traditions, or even just to have someone to talk to as the teacher guides them through discussion prompts. I mean who doesn't love a good old-fashioned pen pal over video? In the following resource, Miller (2020), explains more about Mystery Skypes.

Figure 2.5 *A QR code to Ditch That Textbook: About Mystery Skypes and Why We Need More*

bit.ly/ampglobaledu3

Scan this QR code to see how we have collaborated with friends across the globe.

Figure 2.6 *A QR Code to Going Global with Teams*

bit.ly/ampglobaledu4

A note from Becky: Once relationships or connections are built between two classes in a Mystery Skype, teacher collaboration can take place to bring in Webb's Depth of Knowledge level two, three, and four types of questions. Students can harness their video pen pals to ask authentic questions and engage in inquiry based learning.

Flipgrid

Providing students with authentic opportunities to problem solve, think critically, and make connections can all be done by using Flipgrid. Flipgrid is a FREE interactive video and audio tool that allows students to respond to specific topics provided by the teacher. Students can solve a problem, show steps to a process, interview a classmate or a teacher, explain a project, or even connect with other students from across the globe by using GridPals. The possibilities are endless and vital to the collaborative classroom environment. According to Merrill (2021), we need to provide our students with the opportunity to learn content from authentic real-world experiences to then be able to share with a global audience. This form of learning helps cultivate student engagement. Scan this QR code to learn more about how to incorporate Flipgrid into your classroom lesson design.

Figure 2.7 *A QR Code to Getting Started with Flipgrid*

bit.ly/ampglobaledu5

Flipgrid also offers live events for students to participate in. The events are available on-demand to view at a later time. These events are an excellent way to incorporate real-world experiences for your students such as field trips and author talks. Be sure to check out Lanny's review of Flipgrid!

"Flipgrid not only facilities academic growth, but also provides the perfect environment to nurture citizenship, both within their school community, the community they live in but importantly global citizenship. Connecting classes through topics pupils, can share their diverse cultures, develop friendships, enjoy the things they have in common and celebrate their differences. When we allow our pupils to make this important connection, we are providing them with an opportunity to make friends across the world and allowing them to take the first steps in being the global change makers we wish them to become."

Paul 'Lanny' Watkins (@Lanny_Watkins)

Figure 2.8 *Lanny's Review of Flipgrid*

Scan the QR code below in Figure 2.9 to see a YouTube playlist of Flipgrid Live Events.

Figure 2.9 *A QR Code to Flipgrid Live Events*

bit.ly/ampglobaledu6

BRINGING GAME-BASED LEARNING INTO YOUR CLASSROOM

Within many EdTech circles, game-based learning keeps coming up as a topic. It seems like a concept that many of us understand, right? When we think about it, we can take an educated guess that game-based learning means bringing games into our lesson delivery, because it will engage students and they will connect to the relevant delivery. As Jenallee, we were honored to join our friends from Cy Fair ISD in Texas for their EdTech LIVE event. (If you haven't been to this event, you need to check it out!) The tech team at Cy Fair did an AMAZING job preparing and offering participants a fun day of learning that was full of ingenious ways to use tech in the classroom! In preparing for this event, we researched the "why" behind game-based learning. Our minds were blown by the content we found about why game-based learning should be implemented in our lesson design.

To incorporate game-based learning into the classroom, the lesson designer is required to creatively design content while connecting to relevant topics with meaningful demonstrations of learning. Through exploring gamification in education, we ran across this FANTASTIC Ted Talk by Gabe Zichermann about the concept.

Figure 2.10 *A QR Code to TEDxKids@Brussels -- Gabe Zichermann -- Gamification through Game-based Learning*

bit.ly/ampglobaledu7

Based on Zichermann's Ted Talk, we share some key thoughts, adding to our understanding of this learning concept.

When kids play video games, they are multitasking, communicating, collaborating, problem-solving, strategizing, and more. According to Zichermann and Cunningham (2011), these skills build neuroplasticity, the gray matter in the brain that supports learning. When people learn new skills, like juggling or another language, gray matter appears. This increases fluid intelligence and helps problem-solving. Zichermann and Cunningham (2011) share five things people can do to increase their fluid intelligence, a.k.a. problem-solving skills.

1. Networking
2. Seeking Novelty
3. Challenging Yourself
4. Thinking Creatively
5. Doing Things the Hard Way

Zichermann (2011) explains that all five of these are facilitated in video games. He adds that gaming produces dopamine. As a gamer is challenged while playing, they work hard to overcome challenges and if they are successful, their brain produces dopamine, which induces them to want to keep going back for more of this type of experience.

Zichermann (2011) shares a story about Ananth Pai. Ananth equipped his classroom with video game systems to teach math and reading skills. In 18 weeks, Mr. Pai's class went from below third-grade level to mid-fourth-grade level; the students were given an authentic challenge they were able to relate with! The students commented: 1) Learning is fun and 2) Learning is multiplayer. In what ways can you challenge yourself to bring gamification into your classroom?

 *A note from Matt: There are many types of games teachers can build into their instruction and lesson design. These can be gamified activities that are collaborative. Within student collaboration activities, points can be rewarded for completing tasks that build up to a final instruction goal. An example is the concept of a "Mystery Message"* game that takes students on a quest to solve a secret message. Using Q/R codes students race to the finish. As students solve each station, a message can be deciphered. The final message can lead to a URL or Q/R code of an engaging video or game that can be played on their device as a reward for finishing.

Gaming Examples -- With Minecraft

We are firm believers in adding Minecraft lessons into instruction. Many academic lessons are available on education.minecraft.net. Minecraft can be played individually or as a multiplayer game. Some of the most engaging lessons we have seen involve letting the students create and problem solve in a Minecraft world. Scan this QR code to read a Jenallee blog post about Minecraft in the classroom.

Figure 2.11 *A QR Code to Jenallee - Minecraft Edu Tips & Tricks*

bit.ly/ampglobaledu8

A few other examples of adding game-based learning into the classroom include using tools and sites such as Genially, BreakoutEDU, and SlidesMania (game-based slide decks). We love the gaming aspect that Genially has to offer! Check out their site at https://www.genial.ly/!

A note from Becky: SlidesMania is completely free for teachers and students. Their pre-made game-based slide decks can be utilized by teachers OR students to create digital board games, and students can own their learning by creating games to be played by others.

We are also huge fans of creating breakout lessons in OneNote. Who doesn't love a fun escape room or breakout activity? They are the latest buzz right now not only in the entertainment arena, but also in the #edtech world. A OneNote breakout or escape room is an engaging activity where students interact in a story adventure to solve puzzles and think critically to identify information needed to BREAK OUT. Scan the QR code below to see examples of various breakouts that you can participate in and customize for use in your classroom. You will also have the opportunity to learn how to create one of your very own. Utilize the included *Make It Mine* links to fully customize the content you want your students to learn within an engaging storyline. The adventure in these OneNote breakouts is sure to encourage collaboration, creativity, critical thinking, and communication in your classroom.

Figure 2.12 *A QR Code to Break Out of the Norm: OneNote Breakout Templates*

bit.ly/ampglobaledu

CONCLUSION -- AMPLIFYING LEARNING WITH COLLABORATION

We have discussed a variety of ways that you, as the educator, can learn about your students in order to properly group them, to maximize the learning potential in your classroom environment. A final word from EducationWorld (2019) reinforces the concept: "establishing a culture of collaborative learning is not difficult. Neither is the process a resource-intensive one nor is assessing collaborative learning work difficult. A teacher needs willingness and an open mind to carry it out." Under-standing the strengths of your students and how they work together will enhance learning outcomes. In addition to grouping students based on strengths, we reiterate that you can create authentic learning opportuni-ties for your students by incorporating HyperDocs. HyperDocs allow for students to collaborate, think critically, and problem-solve all within the lesson cycle. It is extremely important to provide students with opportu-nities to form authentic connections. This can be done by using tools such as Flipgrid and participating in virtual field trips and Mystery

Skypes. Creating global connections also helps students develop online safety and etiquette skills. Plus, students can develop a greater sense of empathy for others and an increased awareness of how things may be different from what they are familiar with, and this is okay.

Games are a part of our cultural landscape and they aren't going away. As educators, we must tap into games as a way to connect with our students and relate to their experiences. Gamification brings about collaboration because students find commonality in ways that are meaningful to them. Collaboration involves two or more individuals that come together to understand a common learning concept and complete a common task. Each of the concepts we have discussed will help teachers and students create a learning space that fosters collaboration, relationships, meaningful discussions, and increased engagement. We hope that we have inspired you to go and be a different kind of awesome in your classroom!

EDITORS' CONCLUSION

Collaboration is much deeper than partner work and grouping students for projects. Each of the strategies shared on supporting diverse learners, authentic learning opportunities, audience connections, and gamification can be utilized in the classroom to prepare students for the real world. While collaboration can take place without the use of technology, students benefit when meaningful EdTech is implemented. EdTech supports collaboration, global connections, critical thinking, and much more. A key takeaway from this chapter is that each strategy is not meant to be a "one-and-done" type of activity. After students take the *Strengthfinders* survey, teachers can continue to use student strengths to create intentional groupings throughout the year. HyperDocs and gamification, when used regularly in the classroom, allow learning to take place beyond the four walls of the classroom. Collaboration is vital to student success, and the strategies shared in this chapter will prepare students for life beyond the K-12 classroom.

Key Takeaways & Instructional Implications and Applications

- Intentional collaboration teaches students to understand diverse perspectives and engages students in real-life social scenarios. Students gain skills that are necessary for advancement in education and future employment.
- Integrating strategies for students to learn about themselves and others, such as StregthsFinders surveys, opens the door for students to better support one another and for teachers to intentionally group students.
- EdTech has opened the door to allow for audience connections beyond the four walls of the classroom. Integrating Flipgrid, virtual field trips, and Mystery Skype allows for students to learn from experts and others around the globe.
- Gamification incorporates the 4 Cs of 21st-century learning and fosters a love of learning.

ADDITIONAL EDTECH STRATEGIES FOR STUDENT ENGAGEMENT FROM EDUCATORS AROUND THE WORLD

Jasara Hines, Ph.D. - USA

Using Wakelet for Student Collaboration

Wakelet is an amazing tool that fosters a number of different tenets: collaboration, research, and organization for assignments and projects. This completely free resource allows teachers to archive material and resources for students, share with them, and then have students collaborate with each other on work on their own to add to the collection. Students can use Wakelet to gather resources for projects, activities, and other endeavors. Wakelet is also an excellent way to promote student choice and voice in the classroom!

Yogesh Kumar - India

Teaching and Learning Using Wakelet - Sharing Student Content

Wakelet is a free visual content platform and content creation tool, which can be used easily in the teaching-learning process. Collections or wakes are the content stories; one can make and share them to Wakelet. Each collection can have a cover image and background image related to the topic. The collections provide a variety of options to develop and share the content. Collections could be shared publicly and also can be made privately and hidden. Through collections, one can create or bookmark anything that has an address on the cloud – videos, podcasts, links to websites or blogs, images, PDFs, Microsoft or Google docs, other bookmarks, and even tweets. Collections can be personalized by adding notes, images, PDFs, and also videos can be recorded and saved directly into the collection. At the same time, YouTube links can be added to the Wakelet. In Wakelet, it is easy to save any item from Google Drive and One Drive -- Doc, Sheets, and Slides. One remarkable feature is autosave for students who often forget to save their work. Wakelet with the inbuilt Immersive Reader facilitates non-linguistic representation, ensuring that the information is accessible to all learners.

Wakelet fits within the SAMR model for integration of technology into teaching developed by Dr. Ruben Puentedura. The main points of SAMR model as per Wakelet are as follows:

1. **Substitution:** Students can read an article on Wakelet instead of in class.

2. **Augmentation:** Wakelet allows for multimodality by allowing users to embed images, videos, articles, and more.

3. **Modification:** Students curate information and resources about a specific topic on Wakelet and can share it widely via social media for feedback. Students critically analyze content and research to create an archive for discussion.

4. **Redefinition:** Students have access to real-time collaboration on multimodal content curation.

Amy Storer &

Dyann Wilson --

USA

Using Wakelet for SEL and Counseling

My twin sister and I have been working together since the start of the pandemic to support school counselors in meaningful tech integration for their counseling programs. One of the most impactful tools that we have used is Wakelet. Because of this tool, school counselors all over have been able to truly see what happens when you leverage technology like this collaboratively. We have used Wakelet to create digital/virtual calming rooms. These rooms are places for families, students, and staff members to find tools and strategies for managing emotions and feelings. This has helped us provide counseling resources to our school community and to amplify and build our students' social-emotional learning skills with the activities and resources we've provided.

Chapter 3: Assessment and Feedback Amplified

By: Zach Groshell

United States of America

"By ensuring that feedback is epistemic and interactive, rather than corrective and unidirectional, teachers can better support and empower their students to take ownership of their learning." — Zach Groshell

WHY YOU SHOULD READ THIS CHAPTER

Currently, in education, we are in the age of efficient and effective formative assessment that can be given with the use of EdTech. Zach articulates this well and provides a number of research-based strategies and EdTech integrations to facilitate effective formative assessment and provide feedback within any classroom setting. This chapter depicts a turning point in education because all classroom teachers and school leaders need to be aware the research is overwhelmingly pointing us in the direction of only utilizing formative assessment. Furthermore, throughout the chapter, Zach outlines and summarizes this theme in four major principles to illustrate formative assessment and effective whole class feedback. Then, with each principle, a number of instructional strategies are outlined to amplify instruction related to assessment and feedback.

One of the major themes of the chapter is that if we are going to assess our students, we must do something with the results or they are a waste of time. Therefore, Zach advocates formative assessment as an essential method to drive instruction as well as provide student feedback. If assessments do not give these opportunities to teachers, they are a waste of time.

Last, Zach discusses the notion of delayed grading and creating actionable feedback items for students to reflect upon to provide optimal opportunities for them to learn. Through his practice as an educator and his research, he found that high-quality feedback is interactive and focused on the what, how, and why of the students' performance. However, he does note that we must be aware that we cannot give our students too much feedback at once, which is something we must be cognizant of as teachers.

Overall, this chapter demonstrates a major shift from traditional assessment and feedback practices. It's a game-changing chapter that you can come back to review and find takeaways to amplify your instruction and student learning.

ASSESSMENT AND FEEDBACK AMPLIFIED

"Do I really know enough about the understanding of my pupils to be able to help each of them?" (Black & Wiliam, 2010, p. 87)

I can remember my first day of teaching better than I can remember last Friday's day of teaching. Armed with a fresh certificate, a cursory definition of constructivism, and visions of Pavlov's dog, I found myself completely unprepared to meet the needs of the 25 students who awaited me in that classroom. After several months of trial-and-error learning, or more accurately, *trial-by-fire initiation*, I soon began to realize that while I could sometimes deliver a passable lesson, I hadn't a clue whether or not my students were learning. Without high-quality assessment information, my teaching was blind to the continuous changes in my students' knowledge and skills, and without a feedback strategy, I sensed I was missing opportunities to guide my students towards their full potential.

Eager to emulate what others were doing, I visited a lot of classrooms and asked lots of questions. What I found was quite unexpected. Everyone had a different idea of what constituted high-quality assessment and feedback, and everyone was doing completely different things in their classrooms! Teacher A down the hall would give quizzes at the end of their lessons, while Teacher B started the day with quizzes, while Teacher C didn't believe in quizzes. Teacher D would spend whole nights marking piles of papers with a red pen, while Teacher E had students reflect in small groups about their progress, while for Teacher F, feedback was synonymous with giving praise, points, and grades. Which way was right and who should I copy? My inquiry into the "best practices" of assessment and feedback kept leading me to dead ends, and the findings together seemed too incoherent, too amorphous, to formulate prescriptions for my classroom.

A note from Becky: The practice of observing teachers and inviting teachers into our own classroom should be an ongoing process of learning for educators. EdTech has made teacher observations more equitable because lessons can be recorded and viewed outside of student hours. Zach shared a great example of the impact that teacher observations had on him during his first few years as an educator.

I know now, having engaged in the research a bit more, that there are certain principles that teachers can rely on to guide their decision-making when it comes to assessment, defined here as the systematic collection and review of information to improve learning (Banta et al., 2014) and feedback, or the provision of information about aspects of a student's performance to improve learning (Wisniewski et al., 2020). Had I known four basic principles in particular -- 1. Learning and performance are two different things, 2. Assessments are mostly a waste of time if nobody does anything with the data, 3. High-quality feedback is epistemic and interactive, and 4. Feedback is about improving the learner, not the product -- my trial-and-error learning might have resulted in far fewer errors.

In the next section, there will be a discussion to describe the research behind these four principles, and three assessment and feedback strategies that flow from this research will be presented. The final section will connect the three proposed assessment and feedback strategies with technology integrations that I've personally implemented in my program as a Director of Educational Technology so that you may trial them in your technology-enhanced classroom.

THE RESEARCH AND STRATEGIES

Assessment and feedback have consistently demonstrated large effect sizes in reviews of the literature (Black & Wiliam, 2010; Hattie & Timperley, 2007; Wisniewski et al., 2020), but it is also clear that the effectiveness of an assessment tool or a feedback opportunity ultimately comes down to the quality and context of the implementation (Wiliam, 2012). The four principles outlined in this section are meant to be used by teachers to guide assessment and feedback practices, and they give rise to three instructional strategies: 1. Online Journaling, 2. Individualized and Whole Class Feedback, and 3. Delayed Grading that ultimately deserves a place in every teacher's instructional toolkit.

Principle 1: Learning and Performance Are Two Different Things

A principle that is often overlooked in teaching, but which is absolutely critical to getting assessment and feedback right, is that there is a fundamental difference between learning and performance (Soderstrom & Bjork, 2015). Performance is what teachers observe in the short-term immediately after something is taught, and it is a poor indicator of whether learning, or a persistent change in long-term memory (Kirschner et al., 2006; Mccrea, 2019), has taken place. To illustrate, imagine that you are teaching a student how to thread a needle. You provide a simple description of the goal of the instruction, you demonstrate how to thread a needle while the student observes, and then you have the student perform the skill in front of you with their own thread and needle. After ascertaining that they can do it unassisted, you check the skill off your list, award a "meets expectations" grade in the gradebook, and proceed to teaching another skill. But wait! A month later, when the student is confronted with a sewing challenge, maybe in "the real world" or in someone else's class, the student is not able to replicate the performance that she made a month earlier before your eyes. They have either forgotten how to do it, or perhaps they never fully acquired the skill in the first place. What the teacher assessed in this example wasn't learning, at least not in the sense that the student was able to retain the skill and transfer it to the next sewing activity, but an example of performance.

This difference between learning and performance may at first seem self-evident, but it is not an uncommon occurrence for teachers to test for skills acquisition immediately after instruction only to discover a few weeks later that students' grasp of the skill wasn't as durable or flexible as they had hoped. Principle 1: *Learning and performance are two different things* compels teachers to view student performance that is elicited immediately following instruction as insufficient data for making strong inferences about learning. Rather than giving a single assessment when the content is still fresh in students' minds, teachers should plan to space out assessments over time and regularly check for understanding through a variety of short-cycle formative assessments in order to ascertain long-term learning.

> *"...Teachers should plan to space out assessments over time and regularly check for understanding through a variety of short-cycle formative assessments in order to ascertain long-term learning."*

Principle 2: Assessments Are Mostly a Waste of Time if Nobody Does Anything with Them

Rarely, if ever, is the point of assessment to give an assessment. And yet, students seem to sit through assessments all the time, often in the form of long summative or standardized tests that produce information that neither teachers nor students ever end up *using*. See if you can spot some of the missed opportunities in the following assessment strategy:

1. Ms. Maul teaches the content of Unit 1 over the course of six weeks.
2. At the end of Week 6, she gives students the Unit 1 test.
3. She collects the tests and marks them with a score out of 100.
4. She inputs the scores into the gradebook.
5. She hands the tests back to students well after Unit 1 has ended.
6. Ms. Maul repeats steps 1-5 for Unit 2.

This all-too-familiar assessment ritual can be characterized as "assessment for the sake of assessment" for at least three reasons. The first reason is that the teacher didn't use the assessment information to alter her teaching, perhaps by, for example, re-teaching a set of concepts that the majority of students missed, adding or removing scaffolding for individual learners, or skipping ahead to more challenging content. By the time Ms. Maul was able to review the test so that she could make inferences about Unit 1 learning, Unit 2 was already underway, making it impossible for her to make adjustments to the trajectory of Unit 1. The second reason is that the teacher missed a valuable opportunity to use the test as a vehicle to distribute high-quality feedback. (For what constitutes high-quality feedback, see Principle 3).By only providing a score out of 100, the students received little more than a weak hint at what they might know or not know. Finally, the third reason is that the students were not given the opportunity to respond to the feedback or use the feedback to alter their next performance. Principle 2: *Assessments are mostly a waste of time if nobody does anything with them* compels teachers to scrutinize assessment information in order to make inferences and draw conclusions about learning (Black & Wiliam, 2018), b) to act upon this information whenever possible by modifying instruction, and c) to provide high-quality feedback to students that they can use to move themselves forward.

Principle 3: High-Quality Feedback is Epistemic and Interactive

One of the most important functions of assessments is to facilitate feedback (Donarski, 2020). But what does effective feedback look like? The unsatisfying answer is that there is not one hard and fast rule for what constitutes highly effective feedback. What may work for one student at one point in time may not work for another in a different context (Wiliam & Leahy, 2016). With this caveat in mind, feedback that is high in information, t which addresses the "what," "how," and "why" of a student's performance, but without overloading the student (Shute, 2007), is likely to be more effective than feedback that is low in information (Wisniewski et al., 2020). This low-to-high information continuum is exemplified by Guasch et al.'s feedback model (2013), which divides feedback into three types of feedback loops: Corrective, Suggestive, and Epistemic feedback.

The lowest level of feedback in Guasch et al.'s feedback model (2013), corrective (single-loop) feedback, is simply telling students if they are right or wrong. We often see corrective feedback expressed in classrooms as marks with a red pen or points and scores in an online quiz. Corrective feedback is considered low-information feedback because while students may come away knowing "what" they got wrong, providing corrections tells them little about "why" they were wrong, nor "how" they were wrong, nor "how" they should go about preventing themselves from being wrong again. The next level of feedback is suggestive (double-loop) feedback, when a teacher provides students with advice and information about how the student's performance could be improved, such as, "Adding details in the third paragraph would strengthen your argument," or "Reducing the amount of text and adding photos would improve your slideshow." Suggestive feedback is more effective than corrective feedback because it includes additional information on the "how" of learning to do something, but it is lacking the crucial element of "why." The highest level of feedback, epistemic (i.e., relating to knowledge construction) feedback, requires that the teacher enter into a dialogue with the student so that they may elaborate on the thinking that went into their task performance. A teacher providing epistemic (triple-loop) feedback goes beyond the view of feedback as a one-way transmission of information by probing deeply into the "why" behind a student's thinking and choices (Sadler, 2010), such as, "Why do you think this?" and "Why might A be a better choice than B?"

When Guasch et al. (2013) tested their model by giving each type of feedback to a different group of learners during an online writing task, they found that the effects of corrective and suggestive feedback were much smaller than for the groups that received epistemic feedback. These findings suggest that when teachers pose questions and request explanations and clarifications in a series of meaningful exchanges with students about the material, and when students reciprocate these efforts by thinking about and responding to the feedback (Wiliam, 2016), feedback can lead to learning at a much deeper level than unidirectional forms of feedback that give minimal information (Wisniewski et al., 2020).

Principle 4: Feedback is About Improving the Learner, Not the Product

According to educationist Wiliam (2016), if the feedback does not change the learner in some way, it was probably a waste of time. This might sound obvious, but it is all too easy to mistake improvement in a student's product as evidence that a change has taken place inside of the learner's brain. To illustrate, imagine that students are completing a project-based assessment where they are to design an invention. One 4th grade student, let's call her Tamara, is designing a board game, and her initial design is a rather crude chutes and ladders-style game that she has made out of construction paper. When the teacher, let's call him Mr. Hampton, senses that the product is inadequate, he decides to intervene. There are countless ways that Mr. Hampton could choose to help Tamara that would improve the board game itself, but not Tamara's capacity to design better board games. For example, he could offer a series of low-information corrections and suggestions, such as "trim this" and "put this here," but never discuss with Tamara why the changes ought to be made or how the changes relate to broader principles of board game design (*see* Principle 3: *High-quality feedback is epistemic and interactive*). Should Tamara follow Mr. Hampton's instructions, her board game will improve, but it is unlikely that the provision of this kind of information will improve Tamara. It would be similarly ineffective if Mr. Hampton chose to do most of the work or thinking for the student (Wiliam, 2016), perhaps by putting together some electrical circuits at home and having Tamara attach them to her board game. Even though Tamara's final product has been enhanced with the addition of electronics, leading to a higher score on the rubric, clearly without instructional guidance on how to build an electrical circuit, or how electrical circuits work, Tamara will be unable to make a board game (or anything else) that uses electrical circuits the next time the opportunity presents itself in the future. In many ways, Principle 4: *Feedback is about improving the learner, not the product*, reassures teachers that it may sometimes be reasonable to sacrifice the viability of the final product in order to involve the learner in activities that will improve their learning (i.e., emphasizing process over product; Garcia & Coneway, 2019), such as halting further progress on the product so that the student can benefit from opportunities to practice a subset of skills separately, receive additional instruction, reflect on their feedback, and so on.

Moving Forward with Instructional Strategies

The literature provides additional insights on assessment and feedback that are beyond the scope of this chapter, but these four principles have especially important implications for classroom practice. Let's recap before moving forward. Principle 1 tells us that short-term gains in performance are not always the best indicator of long-term learning, and we should assess accordingly. Principle 2 tells us that assessment information should be acted upon by teachers and students; teachers must use it to adjust their teaching and distribute feedback, and students should interact with the feedback to improve their knowledge and skills. Principle 3 tells us that high-quality feedback involves the learner in a dialogic process of knowledge construction (i.e., an epistemic interaction) about the "what," "how," and "why" of their task performance. Finally, Principle 4 tells us that the focus of feedback should not be on making students' work of higher quality, but to effect a long-lasting change in the students themselves. There are numerous teaching strategies that could be derived from these four principles, but the three that will be examined in the next portion of this chapter are 1. Online Journaling, 2. Individualized and Whole Class Feedback, and 3. Delayed Grading.

Strategy 1: Online Journaling

Online journaling is an assessment strategy that allows teachers to take snapshots of student understanding through the collection of short digital responses (Ostaff, 2020). As evidence of learning is captured in the form of low-stakes journal entries, teachers are able to use this information to plan instruction and to move students' progress forward through whole class and individualized feedback loops (See Strategy 2: *Individualized and whole class feedback*). In addition to online journaling being an assessment tool and a means to deliver feedback systematically, online journaling serves a third important purpose: it is a highly effective form of practice that makes it a learning event unto itself. One of the most compelling and well-evidenced findings from cognitive science research is that when students engage in the cognitively demanding process of retrieval, or the process of drawing knowledge from "inside" their brains so that it is accessible to others on the "outside," the contents of their long-term memories becomes more flexible and longer lasting (Dunlosky et al., 2013; Roediger & Karpicke, 2006). When teachers appreciate that online journaling has both an assessment *of* learning function and an assessment *for* learning function (Yang et al., 2021), they should feel justified in allotting ample time in the schedule for students to generate responses in their journals, perhaps even making online journaling a routine that happens daily (Rosenshine, 2012). To maximize the effectiveness of online journaling, the research reminds us to space out, mix up, and recycle journal prompts (i.e., spacing and interleaving), to vary the journal entry types and prompts, to allow students to generate responses individually and unassisted, and to refrain from asking students to generate responses to prompts for which they have yet to receive some instruction (Agarwal, Roediger, McDaniel, & McDermott, 2011; Bjork & Bjork, 2009; Chen et al., 2018).

 *A note from Becky: Online journaling can also be done in the form of a blog or vlog (video blog) post to allow for an authentic audience or for teachers to respond in a real-world application. Blogs/vlogs also incorporate opportunities for teaching about digital citizenship.*

Strategy 2: Individualized and Whole Class Feedback

Strategy 2 addresses the tension teachers experience between providing individualized feedback (i.e., comments, suggestions, and advice that is personal and tailored to the specific needs of each student) and providing whole class feedback (i.e., techniques for feeding back to all students in the class at the same time; Kime, 2018). While whole class feedback requires substantially less time and effort on the part of the teacher compared to marking 25-30 papers or conferencing with 25-30 individuals, it comes at the expense of individual attention and personalization. At first blush, individualized feedback would appear to be the superior strategy to whole class feedback. For instance, if a student already knows how to make an outline for a five-paragraph essay, it seems inefficient to subject him to additional feedback opportunities around creating outlines when he could be doing something else. However, recent empirical evidence has cast this commonly held assumption into doubt. In an influential report in the UK, Kime (2018) compared the effects of formative written feedback on individual student work to the effects of replacing individual marking with whole class feedback techniques, such as providing feedback live on a document camera. Remarkably, students in the whole class feedback format performed roughly the same as the students in the individual marking feedback format (Kime, 2018). While further study is needed, given the negative impacts of workload demands on teacher burn-out in this profession (Arvidsson et al., 2019), the surprising efficacy of whole class feedback should at the very least compel teachers to cultivate their whole class feedback techniques and to consider how whole class feedback can be used in tandem with conventional individualized feedback techniques.

Strategy 3: Delayed Grading

The third strategy, Delayed Grading, is when a teacher strategically, and temporarily, withholds grades from students until they have engaged with their feedback (Kuepper-Tetzel & Gardner, 2021). As grades alone are not a very effective form of feedback (Guasch et al., 2013; Shute, 2007; Wiliam, 2012), teachers will often pair grades in an online gradebook with descriptive comments, annotations, rubrics, and screen recordings. The problem is, students are often guilty of ignoring the descriptive feedback whenever a grade is awarded (Kuepper-Tetzel & Gardner, 2021). Students who receive an A may see no reason to scrutinize the provided feedback so that they can make changes to their skills and understandings ("I got the highest grade, after all"), and the same goes for the student who sees herself as a B student after receiving a B ("That's good enough for me!"). In some cases, a low grade may end up sending a signal that the learning goal is unattainable, causing the student to reduce aspiration or abandon the goal altogether (Wiliam, 2012; Wiliam & Leahy, 2016). The strategy of delayed grading can help to mitigate some of the issues with online gradebooks, and grading and feedback in general, by removing grades temporarily from the feedback loop and directing students towards the provided feedback so that they may utilize it to improve their knowledge and skills.

Strategy 1	Online Journaling
Strategy 2	Individualized Feedback and Whole Class Feedback
Strategy 3	Delayed Grading

Table 3.1 *List of Strategies in this Chapter*

In summary, Strategy 1: *Online journaling* is a generative activity that produces assessment data on students' knowledge and understanding of the taught material. As students respond to a variety of journal entries individually, teachers should provide students with high-information feedback, such as questions, clarifications, suggestions, and guidance, and revise their teaching based on the incoming data. Strategy 2: *Individualized feedback and whole class feedback* comprises techniques for providing learner-tailored feedback when personalization is required, and whole group feedback when all students could use the same information. Teachers should consider whole class feedback to be a viable alternative to individualized feedback. Lastly, Strategy 3: *Delayed grading* is a procedure that teachers can use to increase students' uptake of feedback by temporarily removing the interference of grades. Before issuing grades, teachers should ensure that the feedback loop is "closed" (Carless, 2019) by confirming that students have engaged with and acted upon the provided feedback. Having described the general principles and research behind these three assessment and feedback strategies, the next step is to illustrate how these strategies can be applied using the affordances of educational technology tools.

STRATEGY INTEGRATION WITH EDTECH TOOLS

While the words "educational technology" can trigger passionate, sometimes polarized, opinions from different people, it is unlikely that most people's first reaction upon hearing these words is to contemplate assessment and feedback strategies. And yet, the potential of technology tools to amplify assessment and feedback practices represents a major justification for the presence of technology in classrooms. While journaling existed long before the advent of tablets and Chromebooks, the first strategy integration, *Online journaling*, describes how journaling can be taken to the next level by allowing students to recall, explain, summarize, map, and draw their learning in multimedia, and for teachers to distribute feedback in equally plentiful ways. The second strategy integration, *Individualized and whole class feedback*, describes the interplay between personalizing feedback for a single student and delivering whole group feedback, with a specific focus on how each can be achieved with the affordances of most learning management systems (LMS). Finally, the third strategy integration, *Delayed grading*, includes recommendations for how to minimize the interference of grades issued in online gradebooks so that students focus more closely on their feedback.

> *"...The potential of technology tools to amplify assessment and feedback practices represents a major justification for the presence of technology in classrooms."*

Strategy Integration 1: Online Journaling

There are many technologies that can be used to facilitate online journaling (i.e., Seesaw, Google Classroom, Canvas Assignments, Moodle Wikis, Seesaw, Book Creator, and OneNote, for example), but journaling can look slightly different depending on the technology. When selecting a journaling platform or app, it is recommended that teachers choose one that will store the journal entries in an organized way, perhaps as a log, stream, or table of contents, so that past entries are always accessible to both teachers and students. To fully take advantage of the strategy of online journaling, teachers will want to choose a platform or app that affords students the ability to submit more than just text and that allows teachers to provide interactive, epistemic feedback (See Principle 3 of this chapter) in a multitude of ways. Submission types that are found across most technologies include the ability to submit text, images, videos, audio, drawings, html embeds, tables, screen recordings, and file attachments. Common feedback options include the teacher's ability to highlight, annotate with drawings and text, circle, strike out, comment, and add attachments such as multimedia comments, rubrics, and screen recordings.

Once an online journaling tool has been selected, teachers will want to ensure that the journal is easily accessible to students by displaying it prominently in the online learning environment. Before any journaling takes place, teachers will want to train students how to use the basic features of the tool, emphasize the purpose of the journal (i.e., for formative assessment, feedback, and practice), and establish the journal as a safe, low-stakes activity where it is okay to make mistakes (Wiliam, 2012). Students should expect that while not all journal entries will be read by the teacher, they are ultimately accountable for doing the cognitive work necessary to demonstrate their learning and to use the feedback provided in the journal to make substantive changes to their knowledge and skills. Teachers will then want to begin planning journaling activities by selecting the journal entry "type" that fits the goals of the lesson. Several of the most researched generative activities from the work of Fiorella and Mayer (2016) and Dunlosky et al. (2013) will be examined here: 1. Free Recall, 2. Explaining and Summarizing, 3. Mapping, and 4. Drawing. As each journal entry type requires different pre-teaching and scaffolding strategies, it is recommended that teachers introduce one journal entry type at a time and try to stick with it for several lessons before changing to a new entry type. As with any new routine, supplying ample guidance during the initial rollout of online journaling is a key to its prolonged success (Clark et al., 2012).

Free Recall

Free recall, also known as a "brain dump," is an open-ended memory-based activity that is perhaps the easiest journal entry type there is to facilitate. All the teacher has to do is pause the lesson to get everyone on their online journals and then prompt learners to write or type everything they can remember from yesterday's lesson into the journal. That's it. Typically, free recall activities should only consist of about five minutes of hard thinking before students are asked to close down their journals and continue the lesson where they left off (Agarwal, 2017). Research has consistently found that free recall improves memory better than most other studied memory techniques (Dunlosky, 2013; Lipowski et al., 2014), and the product that students submit after a so-called "brain dump" session is an invaluable source of information about what students know that can inform next steps in teaching. In the event that a particular student consistently struggles to get their knowledge out during free recall, a simple scaffold that teachers can use is to write a couple of key facts on a sticky note that will assist the student in activating their prior knowledge (aka "cued recall"), and discretely slip it next to them.

Explaining and Summarizing

While free recall is a goal-free, open-ended retrieval activity, this second online journal entry type requires students to journal with a particular goal in mind -- to generate an explanation or a summary that accurately captures the main ideas of the content in the student's own words (Fiorella & Mayer, 2016). Because explaining and summarizing requires students to organize their knowledge in order to answer a predetermined journal prompt (e.g., "Describe the three main causes of the Red Scare" or "Summarize the contents of the film we watched yesterday"), implementation in a classroom requires a bit more guidance and scaffolding than free recall to prevent students from getting stuck and to ensure quality explanations and summaries. Younger learners in particular may need extensive training on how to select and order ideas before they can produce an explanation or a summary that accurately reflects their knowledge (Fiorella & Mayer, 2016).

In addition to text, teachers can allow students to submit their summaries and explanations as video and audio recordings. FlipGrid (*see* Figure 3.1) is one technology that allows students to easily click a button and begin recording a verbal summary or explanation.

Figure 3.1 *QR code of an Example Flipgrid Activity*

qrco.de/ampglobaledu2

Teachers can support students who struggle to record their knowledge live by first having students write their summaries or explanations as text, and then allowing them to read these texts as scripts during their recordings. Another twist is to frame the explaining and summarizing journal entry as an opportunity to teach others, such as, "For today's journal entry you are going to teach me how photosynthesis works."

Teaching others creates an opportunity for the learner to make greater sense of the material by forcing them to explain and summarize in words that can be understood by others (Fiorella & Mayer, 2016) and it may have motivational benefits (Chase et al., 2009).

Mapping

Journaling through mapping is when students are assessed by generating graphical representations of their knowledge, such as creating a concept map of the material where ideas are linked with connecting words. Padlet (*see* Figure 3.2) has a simple concept mapping tool called "Canvas" that allows students to add digital sticky notes that include text, images, videos, links, drawings, and screen recordings onto a shareable wall.

Figure 3.2 *QR Code of an Example of Mapping Format in Padlet*

qrco.de/ampglobaledu3

Once students have created their Padlet, they can share it in their online journal, either by posting the link or by embedding the HTML code into a rich content editor, so that the teacher can access it and provide feedback. Fiorella and Mayer (2016) noted that for mapping to be successful, students will need some pre-training on how to create a concept map and that teachers should consider starting with pre-made mapping templates if students need more support.

Drawing

Drawing is a journal entry type that allows learners to demonstrate their knowledge of the content through illustrations, either on paper or using computer software. When integrating drawing with technology, teachers should check if the journaling platform has built in drawing features and consider if the drawing task would require a stylus, if a finger on a tablet surface will be sufficient, or if it would be better for students to draw on a piece of paper and take a photo of their drawing. Seesaw (*see* Figure 3.3) is a good example of a journaling tool that has the flexibility of allowing students to draw with their digital device or take a photo of a drawing on a piece of paper and upload it to their online journal.

A note from Matt: Online journaling can occur on a wide range of EdTech tools. Beyond the tools discussed by Zach, several other EdTech tools we recommend for online journaling that are Universal Design for Learning (UDL) friendly include Google Docs, Draw and Slides, OneNote, Flipgrid, Pear Deck, Nearpod, Buncee, and Canva.

Figure 3.3 *QR Code of Journal Options in Seesaw*

qrco.de/ampglobaledu4

When considering drawing for assessment, it is important that students do not feel overwhelmed or distracted by the act of drawing. Some students are skilled artists who may waste precious time making their drawings look aesthetically pleasing rather than demonstrating their knowledge. Other students will have weaker drawing skills, to the extent that the mechanics of drawing will impose a heavy burden on limited cognitive resources that will impact their ability to show you what they have learned. For this reason, research recommends that teachers use drawing with caution, and provide multiple scaffolds to ensure that the drawing doesn't hinder the collection of assessment information (Fiorella & Mayer, 2016). Examples of scaffolds include encouraging students to focus on conveying meaning rather than on the aesthetic appeal of the drawing, giving students specific instructions for what to draw, and providing pre-drawn examples on the board that students can copy (Fiorella & Mayer, 2016).

Strategy Integration 2: Individualized and Whole Class Feedback

The iterative nature of feedback coupled with the complexity of the classroom requires teachers to think of individualized feedback and whole class feedback as complementary sets of techniques within a unified feedback strategy. A teacher may find the need to suspend their plan to provide every student with personalized comments when it is discovered that the majority of students are making the same mistake, and a whole class feedback session may lead to a one-on-one conference with a student after the teacher notices a puzzled expression on his face. At the end of the day, the exact ratio of individualized to whole class feedback should be determined through continuous short-cycle formative assessment and the use of professional judgement from a responsive teacher.

Individualized Feedback

Most learning management systems and productivity tools allow teachers to provide individualized feedback in a variety of ways, such as annotating, commenting with audio, video, and text, and attaching items, such as rubrics and screen recordings. While teachers are spoiled for choice when it comes to digital options for individualized feedback, it is important to keep in mind the superiority of high-information, epistemic feedback compared to low-information corrective feedback (*see* Principle 3: *High-quality feedback is epistemic and interactive*) when determining which features to use. Table 3.2 demonstrates how some technology features are more amenable to epistemic feedback, while others are better classified as corrective feedback features unless combined with epistemic feedback features.

Corrective Feedback Features	Epistemic Feedback Features
Highlighter	Text and/or audio comments
Strike out and/or red pen tool	Video recordings
Auto-grading (i.e., online quizzes)	Screen recordings
Points, scores, grades	Rubrics

Table 3.2 *Common LMS Corrective and Epistemic Feedback Features*

Of the technology features listed in the Epistemic column of Table 3.2, the two that seem to be especially useful for delivering information-rich feedback, but may be underutilized by teachers, are rubrics and screen recordings. *Rubrics* allow teachers to distribute individualized feedback that is aligned with assessment criteria, and most learning management systems, such as Canvas, Blackboard, Google Classroom, and Schoology, come equipped with digital rubric builders. Digital rubrics are closer to "live documents" than their paper-pencil equivalents in that they enable teachers to progressively update feedback over the course of a learning period as students make changes to their products. Unlike paper-pencil rubrics, digital rubrics turn receiving feedback into an interactive, dialogic process by allowing students to hold private discussions with their teachers in the rubric's commenting areas. And, unlike paper-pencil rubrics, teachers can embed multimedia messages into digital rubrics, such as instructional videos, screen recordings, and hyperlinked resources that extend students' thinking. Another powerful tool for individualized feedback, *Screen recordings*, allow teachers to record themselves providing feedback about an on-screen piece of work while "live marking" the work with annotation and drawing tools. While most popular screen recording applications, such as Screencast-o-matic or Screencastify, come with robust video editing tools that allow teachers to trim and add transitions/animations to their videos, given the amount of time that is required to record 25-30 personalized screen recordings, teachers may want to consider recording their videos in one take. Simply pull up the first student's work on screen, press Record, highlight a few key aspects of the performance that can be improved, and move on to the next one. Once the screen recording is complete, Screencast-o-matic or Screencastify will generate a link that can be pasted into the assessment's feedback areas for anywhere, anytime viewing by the student.

Whole-Class Feedback

As was mentioned previously in this chapter, whole class feedback can be an effective and efficient way to deliver feedback when specific techniques are employed (Kime, 2018). *Front end feedback* is a whole class feedback technique where the teacher addresses common misconceptions and pitfalls that can happen during learning, perhaps on a document camera or in an instructional video, before students begin their task. For example, if students are learning how to add two-digit numbers with regrouping, the teacher could involve the class in a dialogue about how and why many students tend to forget to regroup 10 tens by adding a one to the hundreds column. In effect, front-end feedback is a form of proactive instruction in which the teacher uses past experiences with students and their subject expertise to anticipate and reduce mistakes before they happen. *Strategic sampling* is when the teacher selects 3-5 pieces of student work at random and then gives suggestions and involves the class in a discussion for how the work can be improved, sometimes "live marking" the work on an interactive whiteboard or a document camera (Kime, 2018). *Register feedback* is similar to strategic sampling, with the only difference being that it is the students who present small portions of their work to the whole class before receiving feedback rather than it being selected and presented by the teacher. Students can project their work with a document camera, or, alternatively, submit their work as a discussion board topic. Figure 3.4 shows an example of how individual discussion boards can be set up by each student using Canvas LMS's Discussions tool so that others can review the work and post replies.

A note from Matt: For both personalized and whole class feedback, teachers can utilize Loom to create easy to view screencasts and Mote for audio feedback. Each tool can be utilized along with the LMS that is being used for the class to provide feedback. Be sure to make the recordings and videos short. From around 30 seconds to 3 minutes and 30 seconds to 1 minute and 30 seconds are the desired lengths for personalized or whole class for video and audio recordings.

Figure 3.4 *QR Code of an Example of Class Discussion Board in Canvas LMS*

qrco.de/ampglobaledu5

Once class discussion boards are set up, teachers can strategically sample from student work and give live feedback, facilitate peer-to-peer feedback in the discussion threads, and require students to submit new iterations of their work so that the class can discuss the changes and celebrate improvements.

Strategy Integration 3: Delayed Grading

Implementing delayed grading is quite simple. For every assignment submission that requires feedback, teachers should provide rich, high-information comments, questions, and suggestions about aspects of the performance, but *hold off* on entering a grade until after the student has engaged with the feedback and used the feedback to move themselves forward. It is only after the student has grappled extensively with their feedback, undergone multiple iterations in their thinking or their product, and has reached the learning goal or the passing standard, that a grade is finally awarded (Kuepper-Tetzel & Gardner, 2021; Wiliam, 2012).

Figure 3.5 *QR Code of an Example Assignment in Canvas LMS*

qrco.de/ampglobaledu6

Figure 3.5 illustrates an example of an assignment designed in Canvas LMS to assess students' writing. The assignment's settings have been configured to allow "Unlimited Attempts" so that students can turn in multiple drafts of their paper. By using technology to replace traditional paper-pencil submissions, students are able to capture chronological, timestamped evidence of each incremental change in their learning. In keeping with the strategy of delayed grading, Figure 3.5 shows that even after four submissions, the grade for the assignment remains blank. This is intentional; research has shown that students can become so fixated on grades that they will disregard or underutilize the descriptive feedback they are provided (Kuepper-Tetzel & Gardner, 2021). As each attempt is submitted, the teacher should use the feedback areas in the assignment to provide epistemic, interactive feedback (e.g., comments, worked examples, and screen recordings) and dedicate class time to activities that direct students towards their feedback. Teachers should consider requiring students to reply to and ask questions about their feedback directly in the learning platform to increase the chances that students fully read and reflect on their feedback. As students and teachers interact with each other in the feedback areas of the assignment, the discussions will be documented within each successive attempt, effectively creating a mini-portfolio of the journey from first to final draft. Once there is evidence that students have succeeded at internalizing and acting upon the provided feedback, the feedback loop can be considered "closed" (Carless, 2019) and the teacher can complete the delayed grading feedback sequence by entering the final grade as per their school's grading policy.

A note from Becky: When utilizing delayed grading, it is important to keep in constant communication with parents/guardians. If students are showcasing their work in a Google Doc, HyperDoc, or other collaborative platform, the work can be shared with parents after the first or second round or feedback is given to students. This invites parents into the learning process.

Conclusion -- Instructional Strategy and EdTech Integration Vignettes

In this section, the integration of technology tools with three instructional strategies was examined in detail with the hope that teachers can begin implementing these strategies in their technology-enhanced classrooms straight away. Online journaling requires teachers to first choose a journaling platform, such as Canvas Assignments, Moodle Wikis, Seesaw, Book Creator, or OneNote, and to facilitate a variety of journaling activities, such as free recall, explaining, summarizing, mapping, and drawing. Individualized feedback can be provided on assessments by using high-information feedback tools such as digital rubrics and screen recordings. Screencastify and Screencast-o-matic are two screen recording tools that allow teachers to upload their screencasts to the cloud for easy sharing by link. Whole class feedback techniques such as front end feedback, strategic sampling, and register feedback can be implemented with a document camera or an interactive whiteboard, or, alternatively, facilitated with online discussion boards. Finally, delayed grading is a strategy that will work with most available online gradebooks and which compels teachers to provide copious amounts of feedback on assessments in the LMS, but to leave grades blank until there is evidence that the feedback has been used and internalized by the student.

CONCLUSION -- ASSESSMENT AND FEEDBACK AMPLIFIED

This chapter began with a vignette about the present author's early-career experiences (and frustrations) with determining an assessment and feedback strategy that moved his students forward. Having reviewed the literature on assessment and feedback, the author identified four principles that have impacted his thinking, three instructional strategies that flow from these principles, and easy-to-implement technology integrations that teachers can use to bring these strategies into their classrooms. The implications of incorporating the recommendations of this chapter into daily practice are many. By incorporating online journaling as a class routine, teachers will initiate an ongoing assessment and feedback cycle that allows them to adapt and respond to the immediate needs of the students in their classrooms. By ensuring that feedback is epistemic and interactive, rather than corrective and unidirectional, teachers can better support and empower their students to take ownership of their learning. Likewise, when teachers blend whole class feedback techniques with individualized techniques, a balance can be achieved between personalized attention and collective progress. Finally, when low-information grades are withheld, and high-information feedback opportunities, such as descriptive comments, digital rubrics, and screen recordings, are emphasized, teachers begin to cultivate communities of life-long learners who attend to the aspects of learning that matter.

"By ensuring that feedback is epistemic and interactive, rather than corrective and unidirectional, teachers can better support and empower their students to take ownership of their learning."

This chapter began with the quote, "Do I really know enough about the understanding of my pupils to be able to help each of them?" (Black & Wiliam, 2010, p. 87). While there are no easy shortcuts or silver bullets that will satisfy a teacher's eternal quest for the answers to this question, hopefully this chapter has demystified some of the complexity behind effective assessment and feedback and provided you with some concrete, actionable techniques to try out, and tweak as you see fit, so that you may amplify assessment and feedback in your context.

EDITORS' CONCLUSION

After reading this chapter, our hope is that you have had the opportunity to reflect on your assessment and feedback practices. Zach provides many research-based strategies that can immediately be implemented within the classroom to help facilitate formative assessment in addition to providing effective feedback to students in an effective and efficient manner. Within his vignettes, he outlines several examples of how assessments and feedback can be conducted and given using mainstream LMS's and EdTech tools.

With many strategies outlined in this chapter, we recommend to 'think less is more' while thinking about assessment and feedback. Whether it's integrating student journaling, delayed grading, or whole class feedback, gradually implement these strategies and integrations outlined in this chapter into the culture of your classroom. Over time, the integration of these strategies with your EdTech tools will make the assessment informative to you and your instructions and your students' learning simultaneously, which is the goal and theme of this chapter.

Ultimately, Zach reminds us that we live in an age of formative assessment. Assessment and feedback practices have been revolutionized by EdTech, which have allowed us to develop and conduct formative assessments in an effective and efficient manner as well as see the results to then do something with them. However, he reminds us that the research-based strategies drive our assessment and feedback practices, which can also optimize our use of EdTech.

Key Takeaways & Instructional Implications and Applications

- Assessments are a waste of time if we do not do anything with them. Use the data derived from assessments to inform instruction and bridge gaps in learning.
- Whole class feedback is much more efficient than personalized individual feedback. To make the feedback even more effective, make it interactive feedback that requires students to do something with the feedback.
- Personalized feedback can be automated using many EdTech tools and LMS's to create whole class feedback.
- Formative assessment with previous content and skill assessment in cycles as well as over time is advantageous to seeing progress over time in addition to at a given point in time.
- Rather than giving a single assessment when the content is still fresh in students' minds, teachers should plan to space out assessments over time and regularly check for understanding through a variety of short-cycle formative assessments in order to ascertain long-term learning.
- Focus feedback on the learner, not the student work product. Therefore, delay final grades and focus on providing students with actionable items to improve and then having students write down how they will make those changes.
- Provide opportunities for students to journal and summarize what they have learned. Concept mapping is another form of summarization to illustrate procedures and systems related to the concepts and skills students learn.

ADDITIONAL EDTECH STRATEGIES FOR STUDENT ASSESSMENT AND FEEDBACK FROM EDUCATORS AROUND THE WORLD

Pilar Hernandez - Mexico

Utilizing Formative.com for Formative Assessment and Feedback

Formative.com has helped a lot in the assessment of my students. Although at first it seemed a bit overwhelming, I took the time to see a few formative assessments already made from its library and on occasion checked its blog for help. This helped me get started and progress in using the platform.

The platform allowed me to easily create assessments, personalize assessments using its visual interface, and provide immediate feedback to communicate with my students during the assessment. It allows us to make easy formative assessments, but it can also make summative ones as well if you would like. Additionally, it detects copying and pasting when the answer is open and it has a free hand writing tool question that helped a lot in my chemistry class to show procedures and calculations.

Last, during 2020 when all my teaching and assessing were done online, it provided me flexibility, ease, and comfort to be able to monitor my students closer and help them when they made mistakes without having to wait until they submitted their work since it syncs live. I cannot recommend it enough!

Becky Young - USA

Mote Has Revolutionized My Feedback to Students

Mote has completely changed how I provide feedback. When I look at how much time I used to spend typing written feedback and then compare it to how quickly I can click the Mote icon and just talk to my students...there is no way I'll go back. With Mote, my students can hear the inflection and tone of my voice. They know that I am taking the time to leave THEM a message because I care about them. It makes the feedback personable, which is essential. And the best part is that students can respond right back to me using Mote (which I highly recommend that all students install on their Chrome profiles as well). If we've learned anything the last few months, the learning location does not have as big of an impact as the quality of relationships formed between the students and the teacher. Mote allows me to continue relationship-building while providing actionable feedback that students can listen to on repeat (view the translation) if needed and then make impactful changes. That is just one use of Mote and that alone is worth it. But wait until you see Mote in Forms, Slides, Google Classroom, and everywhere else!

CONCLUSION -- AMPLIFY LEARNING: A GLOBAL COLLABORATIVE

AMPLIFYING INSTRUCTIONAL DESIGN

Throughout the past three chapters, we have showcased innovative and creative instructional strategies centered around instructional design that have been integrated with EdTech tools to amplify student learning. Each strategy utilized in this book is grounded in research, which gives us confidence that when implemented in your class, the EdTech tool that is being utilized to amplify the strategy will greatly benefit your practice and your students. Throughout this journey, we hope you have learned several strategies and EdTech integrations related to engagement, collaboration, assessment, and feedback to implement within your classroom now and in the future. One of the major purposes and uses of this book and the book series of *Amplify Learning: A Global Collaborative* is to be able to come back time and time again to find strategies and EdTech integrations that can help amplify your instruction in your class.

As we enter this conclusion, we will focus on several key themes of the book and book series in addition to providing avenues for continuing our learning and expanding our professional learning networks. First, we will discuss how the purpose of this book was focused on strategies that can really impact the instructional design of your lesson. Second, we will reiterate how the primary purpose of this book series is to compile instructional strategies and EdTech integrations from a diverse group of educators across the world to amplify learning. Third, one of our goals will be to discuss some recommendations for taking these strategies and integrations and implementing them in your classroom. Fourth, we will be providing avenues for continued learning. We focus on our #AmpGlobalEdu hashtag and opportunities for expanding your professional learning network by connecting with fellow readers, contributing authors, and editors of this book. To finalize this book, both co-editors will provide their final thoughts on the learning journey we have been on as we have navigated the innovative strategies and EdTech integrations from classrooms around the globe. We will be rounding out the conclusion by thanking all of our contributing authors for the amazing work they have provided for this project!

Purpose of This Book and Book Series

The primary goal with this specific book was to provide a vast array of instructional strategies and EdTech integrations to amplify the instructional design of the lessons you provide your students on a daily basis. An assortment of strategies and integrations cover each facet of the traditional lesson structure from activating prior knowledge, formative assessment and feedback, guided practice, and independent and collaborative practice. However, we believe much of what was discussed goes beyond the traditional lesson plan. Discussed was how to establish active overt and covert learning that can take place within any classroom setting. Ultimately, these strategies and EdTech integrations lay the groundwork for your instructional design to take place in online, blended, and traditional in-person classroom settings.

Our goal with this book series is to learn from a vast array of talented and diverse educators around the world and integrate research-based instructional strategies with EdTech to navigate our ever-changing classrooms. Education is currently at a crux of immense change, which requires diverse perspectives to create innovative solutions to solve the everyday challenges we face in classrooms. Ultimately, we hope many of our authors' research and strategy integrations with EdTech tools help educators around the world tackle these challenges.

In addition to using this book to help us learn how to further integrate research-based strategies and EdTech, we wanted to learn from educators around the world. Having a diverse set of contributing authors provides different perspectives from what we would see in our own backyard or national educational system. Seeing different perspectives helps us mold our own practices in our school and classroom, but also helps us develop policies to solve problems in our own communities.

We are in this together as educators. Our classrooms and schools may be located across the globe, but our mission is to help amplify our students' learning. We want to cultivate our classrooms and instruction to be centers for learning. By learning from each other, we will further innovate our practices to put our students, colleagues, and professional learning networks in the best positions to succeed in this ever-changing world.

Taking Your Strategies and EdTech Integrations to Your Classroom and School

At the beginning of this book, we discussed the philosophy of 'think less is more' as a way to integrate the strategies and tools of EdTech that you have learned in this book. We are not asking you to reinvent the wheel. Rather, we are asking you to evaluate each chapter and find one to three strategies at a given time to incorporate into your instruction. The purpose of this is that you can always go back into key chapters if you want to then add additional strategies and integrations in the future. Through this we want you to review the chapters time and time again as there will be times when we will need strategies to focus on engagement and other times we may need our focus to be on feedback. This is the nature of education. Your class may change. A new tool may be introduced. Or, you may feel the need to research and try something new. Ultimately, the book's goal is to be a continued resource for you to utilize and find new instructional and EdTech integrations for your classroom and school.

Building Your Professional Learning Network

We hope that your journey across North America and the globe, through reading this book and the other books of this series, will give you the opportunity to add new ideas and strategies for your classroom that can amplify student learning. We also want this book to support you in building your Professional Learning Network (#PLN). In each contributing author's bio we have included the author's Twitter and/or Instagram handle; please connect with them by sharing ideas, asking questions, and following their upcoming projects. Through social connections, we can ensure that we are taking our professional learning beyond the four walls of our classroom or office. #PLNs allow us to collaborate with creative, innovative educators across time zones, grade levels, and content areas.

EdTech tools will continuously shift and alter over time to better meet the demands of our students. Trying to keep up with these shifts can be taxing and a bit unrealistic, if going at it solo. Join and engage with our global #PLN to take some of the burdens off of you and your team. You've made it this far in reading, so let's make sure the learning journey does not stop here. Whether you are new to social media or have become #EduFamous on Twitter, we are all on this journey to support and amp up learning for students. Let's connect!

Expanding our Community

As you grow your #PLN and connect with the authors in this book, be sure to utilize and share out #AmpGlobalEDU. By including this hashtag, #AmpGlobalEdu, we can easily connect and support one another. We invite you to join past and upcoming podcast episodes, roundtables, panel sessions, Twitter chats, and any of our additional platforms as we dive into a deeper understanding of the EdTech tools and strategies shared in this book along with the new and updated tools and strategies. All sessions, episodes, and chats can be easily accessed by searching for #AmpGlobalEdu on Twitter or Instagram or by adding a column in Tweetdeck for #AmpGlobalEdu. We invite you to join us in our expanding global community!

Final Notes from the Editors

As co-editors and curators of this book and book series, we have enjoyed every minute of working with our contributing authors and compiling this book and book series for educators throughout the world. Take a moment to read our final remarks for this book on *Amplifying Instructional Design* as we tried to bring an innovative group of educators together from across North America and around the world as well as provide our thoughts and analysis of their work in each chapter. As you have been an active learner throughout this book, so have we in the creation of this book. We can guarantee you that many of the strategies and EdTech integrations have also been added to our teaching tool kits as a result of reading each chapter as well as the chapters in our three other books of this book series!

Matthew Rhoads, Ed.D. After spending time reading, curating, editing, and re-reading each of these chapters, what struck me is that there are so many research-driven innovative practices relating to student engagement, collaboration, and assessment and feedback that can be implemented into the instructional design of your lessons. Within the first chapter on engagement, there were several interactive slide strategies using Jamboard, Pear Deck, and Google Slides that provide overt and covert active learning for our students. These strategies and integrations involved Thinking Routines, social-emotional learning, and metacognition. As a practitioner, many of these strategies can really amplify student engagement, participation, and learning within your lessons.

Following the first chapter, I enjoyed the second chapter on collaboration because it first focused on the characteristics of our student grouping. Knowing our students and finding their strengths is essential to grouping them because there must be a balance in our students' skills, strengths, and areas where they can improve to balance our groups during a collaborative task. If there is too much unbalance in our collaborative student groups, there will be too much cognitive load by boredom because the task is too easy for the group, too much discussion beyond the task, group paralysis because the task may be too difficult, or the strengths of our students do not match where the group needs the most support to be successful. This discussion about group composition was key before discussing collaboration strategies.

The collaboration strategies outlined are fun and can be gamified. Jeni Long and Sallee Clark take a deep dive into HyperDocs andt truly go into the entire lesson cycle, which is not usually done when discussing the use of HyperDocs as a medium for student collaboration. Additionally, this chapter focused on the gamification of student collaboration and what it looks like in our modern classrooms. A discussion about how to incorporate video games into a collaborative task was fun and invigorating to read and to think about the opportunities that may provide our students to be engaged and working together!

Last, in the final chapter on assessment and feedback, Zach Groshell's four principles of assessment and feedback lay the foundation for how assessment and feedback can be amplified for our learners in our classrooms. With an emphasis on formative assessment and feedback, there is a focus on the learner and the feedback, which means our learners must be given actionable feedback to make gains as a learner. Throughout this chapter, this theme is emphasized over and over again.

The strategies discussed in the assessment and feedback chapter are game-changing. It first focuses on online journaling that focuses on the metacognition aspect of receiving feedback and formulating action to a focus on whole class feedback. Then, a number of strategies on delayed grading creates an effective and efficient formula to maximizing our formative assessment and feedback. Ultimately, by the end of this final chapter, you will see why we live in the age of formative assessment and feedback. It is a masterful illustration of how assessment and feedback can be done efficiently on the teacher's end as they develop and implement their lessons as well as maximize student learning in a simultaneous fashion.

Becky Lim, M.Ed. It was truly a joy for me to read each chapter and to personally work with each of the individual authors in this book. I am walking away from this book with new tools, strategies, and more importantly, connections. As I continue to work with teachers and in classrooms, I have four amazing resources that I can reach out to for additional support on engagement, collaboration, assessment, and feedback.

In chapter one, Debbie brought in her background of working with elementary students and finding creative ways to engage students. She shared many new uses for EdTech tools. While not every tool was new to me, the way that Debbie used each one was creative and put students first. With a stronger need for inquiry-based learning in all classroom settings, Debbie shared PBL connections to better support student inquiry. While Debbie primarily works with elementary students, the strategies shared can be incorporated into any grade or content area.

Jenallee teamed up beautifully in chapter two to bring their own struggles and strengths into collaboration. Their personalities shined through as they shared their purpose for each strategy, especially around how they brought the StrengthFinders survey into the classroom. Genuine collaboration is well thought out and researched in advance, and Jenallee's expertise did the heavy-lifting necessary for teachers to begin implementing collaborative EdTech strategies into their own classrooms.

Finally, in the third chapter, Zach showcased his expertise and his teaching abroad experience with assessment and feedback. He shared the benefits and consequences of different assessment and feedback strategies that are currently used in the classroom along with new strategies to try. .A key strategy that I walked away from this chapter with was around delayed grading. Zach provides the research, benefit, and how-to for each strategy that he shared. I am genuinely impressed with Zach, Jenallee, and Debbie and look forward to continuing to learn from each of these educational leaders.

FINAL REMARKS ON AMPLIFYING INSTRUCTIONAL DESIGN AND THANK YOU TO THE CONTRIBUTING AUTHORS

We hope this book and each of the included strategies and EdTech tool integrations from educators around the globe in the series of *Amplify Learning: A Global Collaborative* are useful to you. Transforming education by integrating research-based EdTech will be an ongoing effort for us as we learn more research-based strategies and new EdTech tools as we progress into the future. We are excited to have amplified educators' practices and skills from around the world. Each contributing author was selected based on the outstanding work that they are doing in education and every single one of them far exceeded our expectations. Let's turn up the volume and continue sharing, connecting, and collaborating with educators on a global level! We want to continue amping up the voices of educators. To further connect, follow the #AmpGlobalEdu hashtag and check out the www.AmpGlobalEdu.com website to learn more about the book series and additional resources related to this book.

#AMPGLOBALEDU

To our contributing authors in this book on *Amplifying Instructional Design* and the *Amplify Learning: A Global Collaborative* book series, thank you for sharing your expertise and experiences with us and the world. Specifically for this book, thank you to Debbie Tannenbaum, Jeni Long and Sallee Clark, and Zach Groshell for your spectacular and groundbreaking work. Each of you made this book possible. Your research-based EdTech strategies and tools will be used by educators around the globe to better meet students' diverse learning needs and amplify their learning. Your voices and skills deserve to be amplified and we hope this book and *Amplify Learning: A Global Collaborative* book series opens the door for continuous global connections and opportunities.

Thank you,
Matthew Rhoads, Ed.D., and Becky Lim, M.Ed.

REFERENCES

About Mystery Skypes and why we need more. (2020, September 30). Retrieved from https://ditchthattextbook.com/about-mystery-skypeshangouts-and-why-we-need-more/

Agarwal, P. K. (2017). *Brain dumps: A small strategy with a big impact.* https://www.retrievalpractice.org/strategies/2017/free-recall

Arvidsson, I., Leo, U., Larsson, A., Håkansson, C., Persson, R., & Björk, J. (2019). Burnout among school teachers: Quantitative and qualitative results from a follow-up study in southern Sweden. *BMC Public Health*, *19*(1), 1–14. https://doi.org/10.1186/s12889-019-6972-1

REFERENCES

Banta, T. W., Palomba, C. A., & Kinzie, J. (2014). *Assessment essentials: Planning, implementing, and improving assessment in higher education.* John Wiley & Sons, Incorporated.

Bell, K. (2018). *Shake up learning: Practice ideas to move from static to dynamic.* Dave Burgess Publishing.

Bell, K. (2020, April 27). *FREE Interactive Tic-Tac-Toe Choice Board for Google Slides.* Shake Up Learning. Retrieved April 21, 2021, from https://shakeuplearning.com/blog/free-interactive-tic-tac-toe-choice-board-for-google-slides/

Bond, M., & Bedenlier, S. (2019). Facilitating student engagement through educational technology: Towards a conceptual framework. *Journal of Interactive Media in Education, 11*(1), 1-4. https://doi.org/10,5334/jime.528

Bjork, E. L., & Bjork, R. A. (2009). Making things hard on yourself, but in a good way: Creating desirable difficulties to enhance learning. In M. A. Gernsbacher & J. R. Pomerantz (Eds.), *Psychology and the real world: Essays illustrating fundamental contributions to society* (pp. 55–64). Worth Publishers. https://doi.org/10.12968/sece.2018.14.

REFERENCES

Black, P., & Wiliam, D. (2010). Inside the black box: Raising standards through classroom assessment. *Phi Delta Kappan, 92*(1), 81–90. https://doi.org/10.1177/003172171009200119

Black, P., & Wiliam, D. (2018). Classroom assessment and pedagogy. *Assessment in Education: Principles, Policy & Practice, 25*(6), 551–575. https://doi.org/10.1080/0969594X.2018.1441807

Campbell, S. (2017, October 05). 10 simple ways to build a collaborative, successful work environment. Retrieved from https://www.entrepreneur.com/article/302126

Carless, D. (2019). Feedback loops and the longer-term: towards feedback spirals. *Assessment and Evaluation in Higher Education, 44*(5), 705–714. https://doi.org/10.1080/02602938.2018.1531108

Chase, C. C., Chin, D. B., Oppezzo, M. A., & Schwartz, D. L. (2009). Teachable agents and the protégé effect: Increasing the effort towards learning. *Journal of Science Education and Technology, 18*(4), 334–352. https://doi.org/10.1007/s10956-009-9180-4

REFERENCES

Chen, O., Castro-Alonso, J. C., Paas, F., & Sweller, J. (2018). Undesirable difficulty effects in the learning of high-element interactivity materials. In *Frontiers in Psychology* (Vol. 9, Issue AUG). Frontiers Media S.A. https://doi.org/10.3389/fpsyg.2018.01483

Clark, R. E., Kirschner, P. A., & Sweller, J. (2012). *Putting students on the path to learning: The case for fully guided instruction*, 6–11.

Coalition for Psychology in Schools and Education. (2015). Top 20 principles from psychology for Pre K-12 teaching and learning. In *American Psychological Educational Association.*

Dunlosky, J. (2013). Strengthening the student toolbox. *American Educator, 37*(3), 12–21. http://www.aft.org/sites/default/files/periodicals/dunlosky.pdf

Dunlosky, J., Rawson, K. A., Marsh, E. J., Nathan, M. J., & Willingham, D. T. (2013). Improving students' learning with effective learning techniques: Promising directions from cognitive and educational psychology. *Psychological Science in the Public. 14*(1). https://doi.org/10.1177/1529100612453266

EducationWorld. (2019). *Importance of collaborative learning in the classroom.* Retrieved from https://www.educationworld.in/importance-of-collaborative-learning-in-the-classroom/

Fiorella, L., & Mayer, R. E. (2016). Eight ways to promote generative learning. *Educational Psychology Review, 28*(4), 717–741. https://doi.org/10.1007/s10648-015-9348-9

Garcia, B., & Coneway, B. (2019). Appropriate processing time: Valuing process over product. *The European Journal of Educational Sciences, 6*(3). https://doi.org/10.19044/ejes.v6no3a1

Guasch, T., Espasa, A., Alvarez, I. M., & Kirschner, P. A. (2013). Effects of feedback on collaborative writing in an online learning environment. *Distance Education, 34*(3), 324–338. https://doi.org/10.1080/01587919.2013.835772

Haiken, M. (2021). *5 ways to gamify your classroom.* ISTE. Retrieved from https://www.Iste.Org/Explore/In-the-Classroom/5-Ways-to-Gamify-Your-Classroom.

Hammond, Z. L. (2015). *Culturally responsive teaching and the brain.* Corwin.

Harvard Graduate School of Education. (2019). Harvard project zero. In: *sel n.m (eds) encyclopedia of the sciences of learning.* Spring, Boston, MA.

Hattie, J. (2012). *Visible learning for teachers: Maximizing impact on learning.* New York: Routledge.

REFERENCES

Hattie, J., & Timperley, H. (2007). The power of feedback. *Review of Educational Research, 77*(1), 81–112. https://doi.org/10. 3102/003465430298487

Heart Mind Online. (2014). *Boost emotional intelligence with the mood meter.* Heart-Mind Online. Retrieved April 23, 2021, from https:// heartmindonline.org/resources/boost-emotional-intelligence-with-the-mood-meter

Highfill, L., Hilton, K., & Landis, S. (2016). *The Hyperdocs handbook: Digital lesson design using Google Apps.* Elevate Books EDU.

ISTE Standards for Educators. (n.d.). Retrieved from https://www.iste.org/standards/for-educators

Kime, S. (2018). Reducing teacher workload: The 're-balancing feedback' trial. *Digital Education Resource Archive.* Retrieved from https://dera. ioe.ac.uk/31210/

Kirschner, P. A., Sweller, J., & Clark, R. E. (2006). Why minimal guidance during instruction does not work: An analysis of the failure of constructivist, discovery, problem-based, experiential, and inquiry-based teaching. *Educational Psychologist, 41*(2), 75–86. https:// doi.org/10.1207/s15326985ep4102_1

REFERENCES

Kuepper-Tetzel, C. E., & Gardner, P. L. (2021). Effects of temporary mark withholding on academic performance. *Psychology Learning & Teaching*, 20(3). https://doi.org/10. 1177/1475725721999958

Lipowski, S. L., Pyc, M. A., Dunlosky, J., & Rawson, K. A. (2014). Establishing and explaining the testing effect in free recall for young children. *Developmental Psychology*, *50*(4), 994–1000. https://doi.org/10.1037/a0035202

Mccrea, P. (2019). *Learning: What is it and how might we catalyse it?* Ambition Institute. Retrieved from https://www.ambition.org.uk/ research-and-insight/learning-what-is-it/

Merrill, J., & Merrill, K. (2021). *Flipgrid in the Inter-ACTIVE Class: Encouraging inclusion and student voice in the elementary classroom.* Elevate Books Edu.

Miller, M. (2020). *Do more with google classroom: Teacher better. save time. make a difference.* Dave Burgess Consulting: San Diego, CA

Ostaff, C. (2020). *Teaching online handbook.* John Catt Educational LTD.

PBL Works. (2021.). *What is PBL ?* PBL Works. Retrieved 20 April, 2020, from https://www. pblworks.org/what-is-pbl

REFERENCES

Pedler, M., Yeigh, T., & Hudson, S. (2020). The teacher's role in student engagement: A Review. *Australian Journal of Teacher Education, 45*(3), 48-55. http://dx.doi.org/10/14221/ajte.2020v45n3.4

Poth, R. D. (2018). *Collaboration: Bringing students together to promote learning.* Getting Smart. Retrieved from https://www.gettingsmart.com/2018/10/collaboration-bringing-students-together-to-promote-learning-can-move/

Rath, T. (2007). *StrengthsFinder 2.0* (1st ed.). Gallup Press.

Reinken, C. (2012). How to use choice boards to differentiate learning. The art of education university. Retrieved 20 April, 2021.

Responsive Classroom. (2016, June 7). What is a morning meeting? Responsive classroom. Retrieved April 20, 2021, from https://www.responsiveclassroom.org/what-is-morning-meeting/

Ritchhart, R., Church, M., & Morrison, K. (2011). *Making thinking visible.* Jossey Bass Wiley.

REFERENCES

Roediger, Henry & Agarwal, Pooja & Mcdaniel, Mark & McDermott, Kathleen. (2011). Test-enhanced learning in the classroom: Long-term improvements from quizzing. *Journal of Experimental Psychology*. Vol. *17*, p. 382-95. doi: 10.1037/a0026252.

Roediger, H. L., & Karpicke, J. D. (2006). Test-enhanced learning: Taking memory tests improves long-term retention. *Psychological Science, 17*(3), 249–255. https://doi.org/10.1111/j.1467-9280.2006.01693.x

Rosenshine, B. (2012). Principles of instruction: Research-based strategies that all teachers should know. *American Educator*, 12–20. https://doi.org/10.1111/j.1467-8535.2005.00507.x

Ruiz-Primo, M. A., & Furtak, E. M. (2007). Exploring teachers' informal formative assessment practices and students' understanding in the context of scientific inquiry. *Journal of Research in Science Teaching, 44*(1), 57–84. https://doi.org/10.1002/tea.20163

Sadler, D. R. (2010). Beyond feedback: Developing student capability in complex appraisal. *Assessment and Evaluation in Higher Education, 35*(5), 535–550. https://doi.org/10.1080/02602930903541015

Schlechty, P. C. (2011). *Engaging students: The next level of working the work (2nd ed.)* Jossey-Bass.

Shute, V. J. (2007). *Focus on formative feedback.* Retrieved from https://www.ets.org/Media/ Research/pdf/RR-07-11.pdf

Soderstrom, N. C., & Bjork, R. A. (2015). Learning versus performance: An integrative review. *Perspectives on Psychological Science, 10*(2), 176– 199. https://doi.org/10.1177/1745691615569000

Sparks, S. D. (2020). Children must be taught to collaborate, studies say. *Education Week.* https://www.edweek.org/leadership/ children-must-be-taught-to-collaborate- studies-say/2017/05

Spencer, J. (2019, 18 March). *Making the shift from student engagement to student*

empowerment. John Spencer. Retrieved 20 April, 2021, from https://spencerauthor.com/ empowerment-shifts/

Spencer, J. (2020). *Empowered at a distance.* Blend Education

Sweller, J. (1988). Cognitive load during problem- solving: Effects on learning. *Cognitive Science, 12,* 257–285. https://doi.org/10. 1207/s15516709cog1202_4.

Leahy, W., & Sweller, J. (2008). The imagination effect increases with an increased intrinsic cognitive load. *Applied Cognitive Psychology: The Official Journal of the Society for Applied Research in Memory and Cognition, 22*(2), 273-283.

Student Engagement. (2016, February 8). *The glossary of education reform.* Retrieved April 7,2021, from https://www.edglossary.org/student-engagement/

TEDxYouth. (2011, June 09). Retrieved June 01, 2021, from https://www.youtube.com/watch?v=O2N-5maKZ9Q

Trilling, B., & Fadel, C. (2012). *21st century skills: Learning for life in our times* (1st ed.). John Wiley And Sons Inc.

Thomas, J. W. (2000, March). *A review of research on project based learning.* PBL Works, 2-5.

Wiliam, D. (September, 2012). Feedback: Part of a system. *Educational Leadership, 70,* 31–34.

Wiliam, D. (2016). The secret of effective feedback. *Educational Leadership, 73*(7), 10–15.

Wiliam, D., & Leahy, S. (2016). *Embedding formative assessment.* Hawker Brownlow Education.

Wisniewski, B., Zierer, K., & Hattie, J. (2020, January). The power of feedback revisited: A meta-analysis of educational feedback research. *Frontiers in Psychology*, *10*, 1–14. https://doi.org/10.3389/fpsyg.2019.03087

Yale University. (2021). What is RULER? RULER. Retrieved April 23, 2021, from https://www.rulerapproach.org/about/what-is-ruler/

Yang, C., Luo, L., Vadillo, M. A., Yu, R., & Shanks, D. R. (2021). Testing (quizzing) boosts classroom learning: A systematic and meta-analytic review. In *Psychological Bulletin, 2* (99) https://doi.org/10.1037/bul0000309

Zichermann, G., & Cunningham, C. (2011). Gamification by design: Implementing game mechanics in web and mobile apps. Sebastopol, CA: O'Reilly Media.

LIST OF TABLES

LIST OF FIGURES

LIST OF FIGURES

CONTRIBUTING AUTHOR BIOGRAPHIES

Debra Tannenbaum

Debbie Tannenbaum works as an Elementary School Technology Specialist in Fairfax County, VA. An educator with over twenty years of experience, Debbie Tannenbaum supports both staff and students to integrate technology tools into instruction through both co-teaching sessions and weekly technology classes. She is not only a Google Certified Educator, Levels 1 and 2, but is also a Flipgrid Student Voice Ambassador and a Pear Deck Regional Coach. Her first book, *TRANSFORM — Techy Notes to Make Learning Sticky* was published in May 2021 by Road to Awesome LLC. Debbie also blogs and shares her thoughts and reflections regularly on her website: https://www.tannenbaumtech.com. You can also find her on Twitter, Instagram, LinkedIn, and Voxer at @TannenbaumTech.

Jeni Long and Salleé Clarke aka Jenallee

Jeni Long and Salleé Clark are international speakers, EdTech consultants, bloggers, and authors. Between the two of them, they have 37 years of experience in education. They currently serve as Instructional Technologists with Eagle Mountain-Saginaw ISD in Ft Worth, TX.

This dynamic duo, known as Jenallee, is passionate about emPOWERing teachers with technology integration and sharing ways to make learning accessible, equitable, and fun for all! Jeni and Salleé co-host a YouTube show called The Jenallee Show. Their blog and YouTube show highlights the newest EdTech tools and offer tech tutorials for teachers and educators across the globe. Together, Jeni and Salleé are co-authors of the book titled, Microsoft Teams in the EmPOWERed Class. Connect with Jenallee -- bit.ly/jenallee

Zach Groshell

Zach Groshell is the Director of Educational Technology at The Northwest School in Seattle, WA. Previously, he has served as an instructional coach, design technology teacher, and elementary teacher in international schools in Vietnam, Sudan, and China. Zach maintains an active professional presence on Twitter (@mrzachg) and his blog (educationrickshaw.com), and he is an experienced presenter at education conferences. Zach is currently learning how to be a parent while finishing his PhD in Instructional Design for Online Learning. Zach would like to thank his wife, Stephanie, for modeling many of the principles of effective feedback while helping him to improve this book's chapter on effective feedback.

PUBLISHING